For David, Beth, and Heather

Contents

The Creative State

WHAT IS CREATIVITY? Creativity is bringing something new into the world. It is catching and holding fast a fleeting moment of truth in a painting, a piece of clay, or a poem. It is discovering a new interpretation or taking something that already exists and changing it in an unpredictable way.

We often create out of necessity. A table knife or a dime becomes a screwdriver. We create for increased efficiency. Creativity involves a situation we want to change and brings about an enlargement, a progression. What we create is greater than the sum of its parts. The artist's idea, the canvas, the brush, and the paints are not worth a great deal alone. The value is in the finished work.

Our Creative Selves

The ability to create is a basic human trait. Yet often we are afraid to create for fear it will make us appear too different from others, too individualistic. But this fear was instilled in us; children create without self-consciousness. It is only later that they are led to believe that they have to conform to a prosaic world of routine and rigid structure.

Just before rehearsal for *Sugar*, Little Theatre of Tuscarawas County (photo by Bill Douds).

They write stories and draw pictures and pretend to be
other people. For them fantasy and reality often are one.
Many of their creations show how they perceive the world
or how they would like it to be, at least for the moment.
They have the capacity to create and the freedom to do so
because no one has told them they cannot accomplish
what they want. Or at least it hasn't been drummed into
them yet.

Through creativity, children interpret and grow and become more a part of their universe. But as they become
older, they learn to fear. Since creativity is an interpretation of their world, they begin to think: "Maybe the world
is not as I see it. And if I am wrong, people will laugh at
me. What if I make a fool of myself?"

Of course, being creative means exposing ourselves, becoming more vulnerable than we could possibly be in any
other situation. Since it involves a great risk, we have to
learn that having one of our creations rejected does not
mean the end of the world. It does not make us worthless
individuals. Rejection of our creations can cause pain. But
if we learn to view the rejection in its proper perspective, it
can provide us with an excellent learning experience. We
tell ourselves, "All right, maybe what I was doing was not
good, and so I have to change it the next time. Then I'll do
better. I'll learn by my mistakes." Certainly, not all of us
can become painters or architects—at least not on a professional basis. Yet each of us can be creative in a particular
way or in a variety of ways. To be successful we must
believe in ourselves.

Creativity

Creating means believing, dreaming visions, carrying our own pocket of happiness with us. It is allowing ourselves to open up so that we can take in and give forth. It is a feeling of vitality. And once we have completed the creation, it is pride and satisfaction.

In all forms of creativity, the creators reveal themselves. Each creation is a part of us. Each of us is unique. We are all that has formed us into what we are today: memories, genes, experience. We are capable of using all of ourselves, including what is below the conscious level, as tools.

Creativity is being what we can be and allowing ourselves to become. It is interpreting and reinterpreting in the light of the present and future. Were we to create a role in a play at the age of twenty and then create the same role at the age of thirty, we would do it differently. We have different perceptions of the world. Our views constantly change.

In each art form, if the artists are honest they create their own visions of what life is. And when they focus this vision and relate it to the human condition in an equally honest manner, they create truth.

Obviously, the way the interpretations are made differs from one art form to another. But each depiction is valid. And how we use our interpretations within each form determines how successful we are in the eyes of the world.

There are many reasons for being creative. Both as children and adults we use creativity to understand and teach ourselves about our environment. We often can gain a new perspective by viewing a situation through a different point of view. Psychotherapists have us engage in such role-playing to gain insights into our lives. "You be the mother, the teacher, the neighbor," they say, "and I'll be you." So we walk in another's moccasins, at least as much as possible. Of course, we do the same things as actors.

Creativity is a basic human trait; we can all do it. Some of us are better at it than others. And not all of our creations are worth sharing. But we need to find that out for ourselves. If we get into the habit of squelching our ideas because we think they are not worth repeating, then when we create from any idea, in any form, we risk the danger of thinking it worthless or of not even recognizing that we've thought of something new. In brainstorming no idea is judged until the session has ended. We need to brainstorm with ourselves. What we first may have been afraid to acknowledge may turn out to be an idea of worth.

The Creative Personality

What traits do creative persons have in common? First, they have learned to trust their intuitions, to be independent. Of course, they often need reassuring, yet they have learned not only to rely on themselves but to know themselves.

Actress and teacher Maria Ouspenskaya said that a small germ can expand into a great idea. But we have to have the germ inside us and be aware that it is there. And whether a creative person succeeds or not, he or she has to project success or believe it will happen.

Creative persons are questioning, non-accepting. They seek to discover the truth of a situation for themselves. They do not rely on pat answers. They do not expect things to be a certain way. Instead, they acknowledge the way they are, at least until they can be changed. Those who are creative apply new rules to old problems. They have the ability to see a variety of solutions.

Creativity for scientists or artists does not differ but has a common base. It is how this base is developed that determines the direction of the creative efforts. The creative process is similar for all of us.

Approaches to Actor Training

During recent decades much of actor training has come close to psychotherapy because both have similar goals: getting emotions out into the open; getting in touch with self; developing sensitivity and the freedom to be ourselves without being criticized or prejudged.

If we learn to analyze and examine our emotions, then we can use them in our acting. Of course, the neurotic artist or creator is doing the same thing—but for this person the act is a purging, a therapy that becomes almost ritualized in its repetition. It has often been stated that no great masterpieces have been created without the artist's suffering. Like most adages, this one has at least a grain of truth. It is easier to portray depression if you have been depressed. But to create or recreate a feeling in an effective manner, it is better to stand off from that feeling. Then you can analyze it, tear it apart and feel its texture and color. A creative writer often needs to put the novel away for a few weeks to be able to reapproach it in a more effective manner. An actor needs several weeks to build a character, possibly at first with a great portion of instinct, later changing to objective shaping and honing.

The time to feel the emotion in a role is during the early stages of rehearsal. Simply: If you cry, the audience will not. You need to be in control to create effectively. And if

you find, examine, and analyze emotions, this often is
easier to do.

Certainly, people create when they are frustrated or
angry. Sometimes they have to. "The show must go on."
But here another creative attribute comes into use: the
ability to concentrate. Just as people often remark that
their jobs helped get them through difficult periods, concentration in acting can do the same.

This leads to a second similarity between psychotherapy
and acting: the need for the actor to get in touch with self.
"Know thyself" is good advice for any artist. You can
create more easily. You come to know that in dozens of
ways you are like millions of others; in some ways, like
none. What you create will be different from what anyone
else can create. Yet it will be similar. And that is good. A
work of art needs distinction to make it stand out,
similarity for identification. You need to know yourself to
be open to the creative state. The knowledge you gain will
help in the roles you play.

In "The Child and the Shadow," science fiction writer
Ursula LeGuin talks about the balance between
humankind's good and evil selves. She says that as Jung
suggests, we must learn to deal with our shadows. We
must examine the dark side of ourselves, as well as its opposite, to be able to create well.[1] Such an examination
provides our ticket to the "collective unconscious." This in
turn helps us identify with the character we are to portray.

When you are in touch with yourself, you are more likely to be accepting of what you are—your strong points as
well as your limitations. You will have more self-con-
fidence, more trust in your abilities. And it is easier to
create if you are at ease with your creative self.

A third similarity between recent actor training and
psychotherapy is an emphasis on developing sensitivity. In

psychotherapy this means being attuned to our environment and literally involves the physical senses and being
aware of what we perceive through them. But sensitivity
also means being aware of the needs and feelings of others,
as well as of our own. A great deal of what we observe and
take note of is later used in our performances.

In psychotherapy a person learns to accept self. In acting, we need to build our confidence and trust.

When an actor enters the creative state with full concentration, he or she often can transcend. Tony Cortez, a
film, television, and stage actor who has lived in the
United States for decades, still retains a slight Spanish accent in conversation. When he played the attorney in
Miller's A View from the Bridge, a friend asked him when
he had lost his accent. Suddenly, he realized that when he
was playing the part, he had no accent. But offstage it
comes back.

Creativity and Acting

In Creativity in the Theatre, Philip Weissman says that
the end product of an actor's creativity "is ultimately
derived from the unconscious part of the mental ap-
paratus."[2] This means two things. First, the broader the
knowledge we have, the better the source to draw from in
our acting. Second, it means our response is often intuitive.
If we have thought about and concentrated on creating a
character, then we unconsciously draw on our experiences
and background and knowledge in creating a role.

At the same time, actors are more conscious of the workings of their minds. They have, as do other creative people,
a "perceptive openness to [their] inner life, to [their] feelings and emotions, to [their] imagery and symbolic proces-

ses, and to much that in others remains unconscious."3
This is because the creative artist recognizes the need to
"know thyself."

When the time comes to create, the actor can draw upon
stored knowledge, and to a great degree this is intuitive.
He or she can and should analyze characters and roles.
But "an artist who knows absolutely what he is doing, in
absolute detail, is a dead technician."4

Before we can create, we have to have an awareness of
our world. Creative people "trust [their] feelings, [their] intuitions about things; [they] mould sparks of inspiration
that arise from within [themselves] or from the environment."5 Yet this is more likely to happen if we have
planned and have examined the evidence and consciously
sought a solution to our problems.

The wider the base of knowledge, the greater the variety
of character we can play. As part of the preparation for
being able to play diverse roles, actors should condition
themselves to observe people whenever possible and then
to empathize and feel with them. Just like the role-player
in psychotherapy, the actor must learn to see the other
point of view.

As artists, we need to have discipline and control and
yet be free to develop within that control. The dancer has a
repertoire of specific moves, but it is how the moves are
put together, executed, and flow that provides the freedom.
An actor, like any other artist, needs to know technique.
But it is how the technique is used that determines success.

An actor in a play, through the characterization,
presents an illusion of life, but certainly not life. The
portrayal very often is built from the actor's observations
of a combination of people, some of whom the actor does
not even consciously remember. An actor—a real person—
portrays an unreal character (even in a historical play the

characters are merely the writer's conception of the real person) and presents truth through illusion. For if the actors did not present truth, they would not be doing their jobs.

Art imitates life. The actor imitates in presenting the character. But the actor takes from the ones imitated only those things needed to express whatever he or she wants to express. A faithful and total reproduction of life is not art, nor is it even possible to achieve. Instinct and imitation work hand in hand with imagination to create something new. Yet this unique creation often is more truthful than would be a reproduction of actual life because the truth is heightened and sharpened and so brought to the audience much more forcefully.

Just as a child pretends that a stick of wood is a polished sword, so the audience accepts the illusion onstage as real in what poet/critic Samuel Taylor Coleridge called "the willing suspension of disbelief." The truth the theatre artists are communicating and that the audience is accepting is much broader than the "truth" or falsity of an actor in pancake makeup under strong lights in a three-walled room of flimsy canvas. A play communicates universal truth.

Not only is it unworkable to try to transfer life directly to the stage, but the actor must be able to understand which parts of life can be copied and used, and be selective in choosing them. For instance, there are many reactions to grief. A fairly common one is to escape through sleep. But such a reaction may not only be unbelievable, but it could appear ludicrous.

Actors onstage reveal both their talent and their inner selves. Artists can take only what previously has been internalized and externalize it. We create from within what we have synthesized from without. We are like wonderful

computers who are fed information and then spew it forth
in constant answer to the questions life asks us. Each of us
uses the stored information differently. Everything we say,
even by tone of voice and rate of speaking, comes out differently than the way anyone else would say it. As Morris
Carnovsky states: "The actor, like all craftsmen, brings
him Self to the work. He also finds him Self in the work
and he brings back this perpetually renewed Self time
after time, [to] the work."[6]

Philip Burton says actors are those "who find [their] ful-
lest self-realization by imaginatively assuming the being
and actions of fictitious characters for the entertainment of
audiences gathered in a theatre."[7]

But how does one assume these actions, this fictitious
being? Most important, we have to determine through
analysis and imagination what the character is like. And
then we figure out how the character would act and react
as a result of what the person is. Again we internalize and
then externalize. The more artificial the acting, the less we
bring of self to the role.

Just what is it, then, that the audience sees onstage? An
actor, a person, a character developed by the
playwright/performer? It is all of these and more. Edith
Evans once said, "Almost all the parts you play, if they are
well written and if you are suitable to them, you find them,
bits of them, in yourself."[7]

To portray a role we have to identify with the character,
at least to some degree. If the person is too alien to what
we are or especially to what we have observed, we have difficulty assuming the role. For we do have only our experiences and what we can do with them to help us
portray a character. Acting is a balance between character
and self. But it is only self that is acting. For when it comes
right down to it, self is all we have with which to perform.

The sets, the lights, and the costumes, though they establish the mood and provide exposition, really are only accouterments. On the other hand, as actors, as individual selves, we know we really are not the characters we play.

Like the rose, a kiss is a kiss is a kiss. But it is what the kiss means to us personally—not to the character we are playing—that is important. When we kiss the special person in our lives, it is one thing. When we kiss a relative, it is another. The actor on the stage should have the ability not to confuse the meaning behind the onstage kiss with the meaning behind the offstage kiss.

Performers often have difficulty with this concept. In the heyday of Hollywood films before the television age, amidst the glamour and make-believe, one often could pick up a fan magazine and read that so-and-so again fell in love with her leading man. Or such-and-such was divorcing his wife of many years to marry the starlet with whom he played such a touching scene in his last film.

The performer needs to recognize the creation of a role for what it is: art. It is not life and should not be treated as such. There must be a separation, a balance between empathy and aesthetic distance. As actors, we can allow ourselves to feel what the character feels, but we must also be objective about the manner of portrayal, including such things as line projection, blocking, and placement. It is how we view the action we are performing, how we view our creation, that is important in determining our success in conveying the art form to the audience. It is the meaning behind the action.

Often actors protest that they don't "feel" the part or that they are having trouble delivering a particular line because it "isn't the way I would say it." Of course, it isn't. The actor is not portraying self but a character. The actor did not even "think" or compose the lines. The playwright

did. Actors would have a very limited scope if they played
only characters who felt and spoke as they do.

Exercises

1. Listen to a recording of instrumental music. What
colors does the music suggest? How are these changing
colors related to your emotions? What are your emotions
as you hear the music? Observe how they change, intensify, abate, become something else entirely.

2. Using pastels, paints, crayons, or colored pencils, listen to another recording of instrumental music and do a
nonrealistic sketch, choosing appropriate colors to match
each change in mood and emotion.

3. James Thurber wrote a short story, "The Secret Life
of Walter Mitty," in which the central character leads a life
of fantasy. In his mind he performs many gallant deeds
and is a great hero rather than the henpecked husband of
his real life. Everyone has fantasies. They are evidence of
your creativity at work. Spend some time exploring one of
your fantasies and developing it.

4. Creativity in acting is determined to a certain extent
by what other actors do, as well as how they do it. Work in
pairs. One member should think of a beginning line. It can
be anything at all. In front of the class begin an exchange
based on this line. One partner should react to the line,
and the other then react to the reaction, and so on. In es-
sence, this is a kind of improvisation. But don't try to
make it go any particular direction or reach any stopping
point. Have at least ten exchanges of dialogue before you
stop. Someone else should keep track. Say the first thing
that comes to mind, whether or not it seems appropriate.

5. Find a partner. One of you should lie on your back
and close your eyes. Then try to hear all the sounds
around you. Determine what they are. Your partner will in-

dicate when two minutes is up. Now switch and have the
partner listen for two minutes.

6. This is similar to the last two exercises. Close your
eyes and try to determine as many physical sensations as
you can: how your shoes fit, how your clothes feel around
your waist and neck, any pressure being exerted on your
body, or any other sensations. Work in pairs. One person
concentrates while the other counts two minutes. Then
switch.

7. For the next two or three weeks, try to discover and
list something you haven't seen before on the way to class
or work or on another route you take every day. Look for
things that are a lasting or at least a seasonal part of the
environment.

8. Begin to keep a character file. Just as you did in the
last exercise, observe a new person each day and briefly
describe him or her in a notebook or card file. In particular, note any unusual traits or interesting characteristics that could provide a starting point for developing a
character onstage.

9. Using one of the people about whom you have written
a character sketch, develop a fictitious character you can
portray in an improvisation. Get together with someone
else in class, and in character talk for one or two minutes,
using a subject you've agreed on ahead of time.

10. Write out the traits you would find most desirable in
a friend. Trade papers with a partner. Now develop a
character based on each other's list. Present an improvisation, about two minutes long, playing each other's characters, who happen to meet at a place you both choose.

The purpose of these exercises is to help you develop
your sensitivity, your sense of awareness. From these two

traits you then have a wealth of information from which to
draw for your acting.

NOTES

1. Ursula K. LeGuin, "The Child and the Shadow," *The Language Of
the Night*, (New York: Berkley Publishing Corp., 1982, reprinted from
G. P. Putnam Sons edition, 1979; taken from a previous article appearing in the *Quarterly Journal of the Library of Congress* 32 (April 1975):
55.
2. Philip Weissman, *Creativity in the Theatre*, (New York: Basic Books,
Inc., Publishers, 1965), 7.
3. Robert H. McKim, *Experiences in Visual Thinking*, (Monterey, CA:
Brooks/Cole Publishing Co., 1972), 30.
4. Paul Smith, ed. *Creativity: An Examination of theCreative Process*,
(New York: Hastings House Publishers, 1959), 23-24.
5. Harold A. Rothbart, *Cybernetic Creativity*, (New York: Robert
Speller & Sons, Publishers, Inc., 1972), 3.
6. Morris Carnovsky, "Designs for Acting: The Question of Technique," *Theatre in the Twentieth Century*, ed. Robert Corrigan (New
York: Grove Press, Inc., 1963), 150.
7. Philip Burton, *Early Doors: My Life and the Theatre*, (New York:
The Dial Press, Inc., 1969), 165.
8. Hal Burton, *Great Acting*, (New York: Bonanza Books, 1967), 129.

Creative Concentration

IT'S DIFFICULT TO CREATE when we are tense because our energies and our mental processes both contribute to maintaining the state we are in. As artist Robert H. McKim says, "relaxation and attention are two sides of the same paradoxical coin...By relaxing irrelevant tension, the individual releases full energy and attention to the task at hand."[1]

Whether we think of the state of relaxed attention as paradoxical or not, it is necessary to creativity. It means ridding ourselves of unnecessary attention and focusing our energies.

We've all experienced doing some mechanical task while our minds were miles away. There is the theory that the soul is responsible for creative thought, while the rest of the mind, the merely physical, is put on a kind of automatic pilot. Who, for instance, hasn't suddenly "awakened" while driving or riding in a car to discover they are miles from the last remembered location?

At its worst this is the kind of thing that can happen to an actor who has performed the same role over and over. The creation has become a craft rather than an art. Ob-

Long Day's Journey Into Night, directed by Bedford Thurman at Kent State University (photo by C. James Gleason).

viously, when this happens, we are relaxed but certainly
are not concentrating fully on the task at hand.

Such a function works both for and against us. In
everyday life it frees our minds of mundane tasks. In the
theatre, however, the actor should stay in touch with the
changing nuances of each performance: the feedback from
the audience, the slight changes in reaction and delivery of
the other actors, the changing dimensions of the unfolding
presentation. The performing artist creates for the moment and needs to be aware. The performance that lacks
the creative spark is a result of the logical left brain doing
its work, while the right brain wanders into new space and
realities. This if fine if the task we are performing actually
is mundane and automatic. But a play is constantly changing. No performance is exactly like any other because of
the moods and feelings of the performers and the reactions
of the audience. The actor needs to be attentive to the
changes, or the performance will falter.

It is paradoxical that we need to be in the creative state
when interpreting character and relating to the changing
patterns of a performance; yet, the very repetitiveness of a
performance blocks our creativity as actors. We need a
balance—relaxation and concentration. We need to view
our performance with both an analytical and a creative
frame of mind.

Music can also help us understand the difference. If we
listen to an instrumental solo, we can get caught up in the
mood and the beauty of the sound. It touches our emotions. We hear with our hearts rather than with our
minds. On the other hand, if we've studied music, we can
analyze what we hear in terms of the mathematics of the
rhythm, the intervals, the progression.

When we as actors are in rehearsal for a play, we need
to be able to shift into the creative state, where we are

open to ideas and images without censoring our thoughts. As Harman and Rheingold say: "The ability to imagine, to conjure up images or visions of things different from our ordinary reality, has always been recognized as the hallmark of the innovative mind. And if we learn how better to imagine or see images, we have taken the major step toward becoming more creative."[2]

Part of this, of course, depends on our not censoring our thoughts, on our being in such a state of relaxation that we are not fearful or tense about experimenting. Certainly, we're going to try things that do not please either the director or ourselves. But not only do we learn by such small failures, but we gain more confidence in ourselves as artists.

If we are anxious, it is much more likely that we will not even attempt to experiment with an action or a tone of voice. Rather we will take the safe route and so limit our communication. There will be fewer subtleties; our performances may still be good, but they probably will not be outstanding. If we feel free to experiment broadly throughout the early stages of the rehearsal and more precisely afterwards, then we have the chance to bring a dimension to our roles that would be otherwise impossible. Such relaxation, in other words, is conducive to concentration.

There needs to be a balance between the logical and the creative. We need to be creative in developing a role, but logical as well since we are using words, at least in part, to convey the sense of a character or a scene. We most often think in words. This means that our logical and creative selves are concurrently in operation, even though we may be using one more than the other. When we are creating, we don't want to be slowed down by minor details.

Creative Atmosphere

There are any number of ways to establish a proper
frame of mind for creating. In *The Writer's Survival
Guide*, Jean and Veryl Rosenbaum suggest meditation. Actually, we can repeat any neutral word over and over to
bring about a state of relaxation. If we take a few minutes
to clear our mind of nonessentials or nonrelated clutter,
there is a double benefit. We can more fully relax because
we aren't bothered by outside noise or worries, and we are
more able to concentrate.

Another technique is to transport ourselves mentally to
soothing environments where we can almost feel the tension drain from us. It could be a spot on the bank of a
meandering stream in the cool shade of leafy trees. When
we lean against the rough bark of a maple, stretch out our
legs, and watch the water ripple over mossy stones and fal-
len logs, we can experience a sense of tranquillity. If we
allow it, we can almost smell the rotting leaves and the
dank odor of mushrooms.

Of course, the spot should be one of your own creation,
such as that described by writer and artist Edee Suslick.
As a child in St. Louis, she found an area of tall bushes.
Pushing her way through them, she discovered an open
space, another world, unexplored and new. She claimed it
as her own, never throughout her childhood telling
another person about it, disappearing into it as if off the
face of the earth for hours at a time. Nearby, workers were
erecting a theatre building, so she begged scraps of lumber
and bricks from them. Out of these she constructed a
makeshift desk and stool. Once inside her protective circle,
she existed in a timeless dimension where she was free to
do as she pleased. The area became both her physical and
spiritual retreat.

A further method of relaxing and blocking out worries is to learn to analyze your feelings. If you can trace anger or depression to a particular base, half the battle is won because then you can put problems in perspective and see that they usually are not insurmountable. Through the analysis you are determining what makes you behave as you do and what your reactions are to various situations. This has the added benefit of showing you how a character in a play might be affected by a similar situation.

Oscar Wilde said there are two great tragedies in life: *not* getting what we want and *getting* what we want. Of course, that depends somewhat on our goals. But usually it is the way we react to life that determines how happy we will be. There is a certain truth to happiness being equated with whether we view a glass as half full or half empty. It is easier to create when we feel good emotionally and are not overburdened with worries and problems. Life depends in large part on how we approach it, and the approach determines to a great degree how creative we will be.

Certainly, people create when they are depressed, but negative feelings are destructive. They feed upon themselves and leave us empty rather than filled with a sense of joyfulness and well being. It is much easier to create consistently and well when our approach to life is positive.

According to Bill Downey, "our creativity appears more frequently when there is less stress...when the mind is suspended from surrounding distractions."³

Hobbies can help us relax and enter into a creative state. So can indulging ourselves in fantasies. The more we create in our minds, the easier it becomes to relax and enter into the creative state, which actually is a state of altered consciousness. Then we are open to all stimuli that will help us follow through with our creations, whether they involve playing a part or writing a story.

Remember that when you are tense, it is difficult to concentrate, difficult even to feel anything except the tension. As an actor developing a role, you do need to feel.

Exercises to Aid Creativity

It is helpful to devote five or ten minutes to relaxation exercises at the beginning of each class period as a shortcut to creating a character or a scene convincingly. Each of us will develop favorites, so it might be helpful to have a different student lead whatever exercises he or she chooses for that day.

For instance, stretching the muscles in your legs can help you relax. Stretch one leg in back and the other in front, bent at the knee. Reverse the process. If you feel tension in your neck, which is quite common, do neck rolls. Gently roll your head over one shoulder, around back and then in the front, letting it hang limp. Then reverse the direction.

One of the simplest exercises is one we often do without much thought: yawning and stretching. Another is to hunch your shoulders up. Move them forward, to the middle once more and then to the back. Massaging your neck with downward strokes can also help you relax.

Different people feel tight in different parts of the body. Some feel it in the neck and shoulders, others in the stomach muscles and so on. Once you isolate your areas of tension, you can begin to relax them. Often it's as simple as locating the area, making it as tense as possible and then quickly letting go.

On the other hand, you can sometimes use a particular type of tension to develop a role. Suppose you are playing someone with an injured leg such as Paul the puppeteer in the musical *Carnival*. You might tense the muscles in the knee to inhibit mobility and then practice walking this way. Or, if your character is one who has a very straight posture, you might experiment with tensing the back. Remember how this affected your feelings and the dimensions it added to the role. Then maintain the attitude and posture without the tension.

People who are uptight tend to communicate their feelings to those around them. If you are tense while performing or rehearsing, it can have an adverse effect on the other actors sharing the scene. Acting is usually done as part of an ensemble. So you affect not only yourself, but the other performers and the audience as well.

The more relaxed you are, the less your technique will be communicated. The best performances are those that appear effortless. Unlike a tightrope walker or a juggler, who wants to make a particular trick seem difficult in order to create dramatic tension, the actor should not call attention to his or her craft. Rather the audience's concentration should be on the meaning, the characters themselves, and the situation.

Instead of transmitting your "uptightness" to others, try transferring it to objects with which you come in contact—a doorknob, a prop, a railing. Visualize the tension flowing from you to the object.

The following also can help you relax:

1. Pretend your arms are ropes, uncoiled at the ends to form your fingers. Allow them to hang loose and then shake them. "Transfer" the tension from other parts of your body to the ends of your fingers. If, for instance, your

shoulders are tense, allow the tension to flow down the arms and wrists to the hands. Then shake it away as you'd shake dust from a throw rug.

2. Tense your feet and toes and then let them relax. Try this with your stomach muscles, your shoulders and back, your thighs and pelvis. A variation is to let yourself droop suddenly at the waist.

3. Stand with your legs apart. Spread your fingers, stand on your toes and reach for the ceiling. Then let your arms fall limp, your feet flat. Now stretch once more. With your arms in the air, hold your head straight, eyes ahead. Feel the alignment of your back. Relax, stretch, and relax.

4. Lie flat on your back. Stretch your arms out at right angles from your sides and spread your legs into a "V" shape until you become a five-pointed star. Inhale deeply. As you exhale, imagine the tension flowing from every point of the star. Do this until all the tension has vanished. Now open each of the five areas to the energy of the earth. Let it flow in and throughout your body as you inhale.

5. Go on a voyage through your bloodstream. Enter wherever you wish, but take with you a magic purifying agent that restores energy at the same time it rids the body of tension. Travel through your arms and legs, the chambers of your heart, the electrical circuitry of your brain. When the journey is complete, exit and begin to create.

6. Feel in your mind each part of your body; examine its functions. Be aware of what each does and how all the parts fit together. Imagine their separate vibrations. Now harmonize these vibrations until you can feel them work together to give you strength.

7. Become a limp balloon. Then, with increased air intake, gradually begin to inflate. Inhale slowly and as deeply as you can until you feel the space around you begin to

diminish. Fill a room, a house, a mountain, a solar system, and a universe. When you have inhaled as deeply as you can, slowly begin to shrink. As the last of the air leaves your body, become limp until you have no control over your muscles and you fall back in your chair or sink to the floor.

8. Make a tight ball of your body and begin to rock back and forth on your back, like a small, round pebble moved back and forth in a gently lapping wave.

The best thing about exercises such as these is that you can make of them what you wish. They stretch the imagination and set it free as they relieve tension and help you concentrate.

As McKim says, an "uptight body" leads to "uptight thoughts." Creative concentration, unlike the kind needed to balance a budget or read a physics text, calls for flights of fancy. For this reason the state may be easy to achieve but difficult to maintain. We've been warned against it all our lives. We've been told to concentrate on fulfilling whatever task is assigned us, and most often these tasks involve precise steps or logical sequencing. In artistic attention, we are free to devote ourselves to fantasizing or fanciful thinking.

The Value of Creative Concentration

When we give ourselves over most fully to our creativity, to the transcendence of self, we probably are the most joyful—but we realize it only in those brief moments of self-awareness when we think of the joy. In playing a highly emotional or difficult scene, an actor is more apt to do well if he or she is not concerned with or thinking of self.

Rather the attention and concentration are centered on
the interpretation of the written part. The actor who stops
to think of technique will in all probability begin to falter
in the presentation.

The following exercises will help develop your concentration, while at the same time they can help develop your
memorization skills. Try these and then develop some exercises of your own.

1. There's an old game that can help develop concentration and memory. One person says, "I'm going on a vaca-
tion, and I'm taking with me..." The object has to be
something that begins with the letter "A." The next person repeats what the first has said and adds something
that begins with the letter "B." The game can be continued through the alphabet as many times as the players
are able to remember the answers.

2. A similar game that probably takes more concentration is played following a four-beat measured rhythm.
Choose a category such as film stars, vegetables, or song tit-
les. On the first beat slap your hands against your thighs.
On the second beat, clap your hands. On the third, snap
the fingers of your left hand. On the fourth snap the
fingers of the right hand and say a word beginning with
the letter "A" that fits into the chosen category. The
second person maintains the rhythm, and on the fourth
beat of the second measure says a word that begins with
the letter "B" and so on.

3. Any exercises in description also will help in learning
concentration. For instance, observe another class member
for sixty seconds. Turn away from the person and then tell
as much about his or her appearance as possible, from
physical characteristics to clothing. Or look at a landscape
painting, turn away and describe it in detail.

4. Try to count to one hundred by fours or sixes while two or three classmates are doing their best to distract you. Those doing the distracting should remember that it is relatively easy to concentrate in a general hubbub; this sort of interference can be blocked out with little effort. But if someone is talking quietly into your ear, concentration is much more difficult.

5. Read a newspaper story aloud while someone is telling you an entirely different story. At the end summarize what you read and also tell the story you heard.

6. Rub your belly and pat your head. At the end of ten seconds switch to patting your belly and rubbing your head. At the end of another ten seconds switch once more. Have someone call the times for you.

7. Do a mirror exercise. Stand facing a classmate and try to duplicate his or her movements exactly as would be seen in a mirror. Halfway through the exercise, switch. You lead and have the other person follow, but do not make the switch apparent. At first make the movements smooth and fluid, increasing in difficulty after you've done the exercise two or three times. As mentioned, acting is usually an ensemble exercise, so get into the habit of helping your partner. If he or she looks bad, you will too.

8. A similar exercise is to have one person tell a story while the other tries to say the words of the story simultaneously. The second person should not know ahead of time what the first is going to say.

9. Before you go to sleep try to remember one thing that happened today, one yesterday, one the day before, stretching back for the past two weeks.

10. Play the game of "Murder." Sit in a circle. Your instructor will have you choose slips of paper. On one is the letter "M" for Murderer. On the others is "V" for Victim. The object is for the murderer to "kill" the victims before

they catch him or her. The victims, of course, want to stay
alive. The murderer kills the victims by winking at them.
As soon as the victims see the murderer wink at them,
they have to lower their heads and not make eye contact
with anyone else. The victims, while trying not to be killed,
attempt to catch the murderer winking at someone else. If
they do, they say, "I accuse [the person's name] of murder." The victim who solves the mystery wins. If no one
catches the murderer, he or she wins. If you falsely accuse
someone of murder, the penalty is "death."

     11. Divide into equal sides and play a game of charades.

     Theatrical concentration is different from the concentra-
tion it takes, for instance, to solve a difficult math problem
or to complete a puzzle. In the latter you need be aware
only of the task. But in performing there are circles of concentration. The first is your relationship with the other
person or persons on stage. Second is your relationship
with the set and the play as a whole. Third is your ability
to communicate the overall sense and meaning of the play.
And finally, there's the audience.

     At any given time one of these will require more con-
centration than another. In the matter of sightlines and
positioning, you are concentrating on presenting a pleasing
picture to the audience. At the same time you need to be
aware of any changes in the play's direction. It is a rare
performance that has no hitches. If an actor forgets lines,
you must be aware of what is happening outside of yourself and your own concerns in order to cover for the person. If you are concentrating only on your own little circle
of dialogue or movement, you are probably in trouble.

     In a dramatic scene where you have a major part, you
will concentrate most fully on communicating your lines
and character, but you must be aware of the other ele-

ments of the production as well. Again, remember that the actor who concentrates most on self usually will not give an effective performance. You need to actually look and listen to the progress of the play and not rely on what you expect it to be.

The Creative Attitude

Creating as an actor involves both introspection and "outrospection." We often examine our own lives for the basis of our creation, but then we concentrate on the theme, the characters, the situation, to the exclusion of awareness of self. We often take things from our pasts and relate them to the world at large. We take a statement that is very personal, relate it to the character we're playing and give it meaning for other people. We take what is ours internally, then change it and give it meaning for an audience.

It's been said many times that nobody can teach us how to create, whatever the art form. Others can provide technique, but the germ of creativity, the talent, cannot come from without. Others can lend us the emery cloth to smooth rough edges, but nobody else can instill in us either the desire or ability to portray a role. We have to believe in and trust ourselves, and only then can we become good actors.

In other words, creativity depends to a great extent on attitude. We need to be attuned to our originality, our uniqueness, and build on it without worrying how well we match anyone else. And if we fail, we can use the failures as stepping stones to success. If you believe you'll become creative, most likely you will.

This is not to say that people can don creative talents or abilities like putting on a suit of clothing. Rather, you can learn to exercise and use what creative abilities you have if you believe in yourself.

Generally, the most successful actor is the one who believes he or she will be successful and improve. If we try our best, we should be satisfied with the results. At the same time we should recognize that our work will steadily improve, and improvement takes hard work. We shouldn't worry, particularly during the early stages of our development, whether we yet are "successful" in the eyes of the world.

We must believe that our ideas and insights are valuable and have meaning. Then we are more likely to pay attention to the ideas and thoughts we have, rather than ignoring them.

If we do maintain the proper frame of mind for fostering creativity, we will pay attention to our hunches and intuitions, which most often are based on reality but stay below the level of our consciousness. Our minds, both on the conscious and unconscious levels, take bits and pieces and fit them together to form wholes.

Our intuitions also can often tell us whether something is "right" or "good." So we first have to learn to trust ourselves and pay attention. We develop heightened perception.

If we listen to our own feelings about our creativity, we are more likely to do what is right for us. Our inner beings will tell us if something does not quite fit. When it does fit, we experience joyfulness. If we feel this joy, we know we're on the right track.

In many ways we need a child's spontaneity. We need to approach the world with a child's sense of wonder. We need to view each day as a new beginning that we can approach with anticipation.

Because each day is new, we approach it with spontaneity, a reliance on intuition rather than on old patterns. For what is creativity in the arts but an interpretation of what we perceive? And to experience and interpret anew, we must see anew.

1. Lean back in a comfortable chair and close your eyes. Become in your imagination a curled leaf on a gently lapping wave at the edge of a mountain stream. Warm sun shines in mottled patterns through summer branches of trees. Warm and secure, you're lulled slowly back and forth. You feel a gentle breeze that pushes you into the current. Slowly, slowly, slowly, you're carried between the banks of the river, through farmlands and forests and towns. Keep track of what you see. Use one part of it as the basis of a vignette, a story, a poem.

2. Now become that same leaf the river deposits into the sea. Suddenly you're picked up by a tsunami, a giant wave, that roars and thunders its way across the ocean. Along the way you see first small boats and then ships being tossed hither and yon. You crash along in the clutch of intense fury that slowly abates, a wild stallion gentled to the saddle and reins. With the touch of a feather you're carried up the beach of a strange island or peninsula or continent. What do you see there? What is it like? Use this experience on the sea or on the land as the basis for a piece of writing, a drawing, or a scene in a play.

If you allow yourself the freedom to be carried along in your imagination, you can go anywhere you wish. A stream or a train can carry you back through the years to your childhood. What do you see? Where do you want to stop? Along the way observe the adult, the teenager, the child, the toddler you were at important points on the journey. Remain the passenger carried along; stand apart from the person you were, yet let a part of you be that person. Stay at each stop as long as you wish; go on whenever you want.

Use whatever device you wish to carry you backward or forward and to other places and times, to new dimensions. Visit a planet. Fly through the fires of the sun. Experiment with destinations and modes of travel. Be joyful along the way.

Listen to a record or tape, body relaxed and eyes closed. Allow the music to take you where it will. When your mind is stimulated by an idea, explode like a bomb of ideas and write them down before they get away.

Because it is easier to create whenever you have good feelings, take a trip into your mind and observe all the things and people you love. Linger a moment with each of them. Reassure them your love is still real. Tell them you care about them, that they're important to you. Allow them to reassure you.

1. Visit your mind once more. Go back through the years to find someone from the past, outside of your family, whom you loved the most. If you never told the person—a teacher, a scoutmaster, the mom or dad or grandparent of a friend—how much you care about them, do so now. How do they feel about knowing? How do you feel? Write a poem or a story about a long-after meeting with someone you loved. Or would like to have loved. Maybe the person isn't real but is a composite of all the things you like in a human being.

2. Now journey back to a happy time—a week ago, a year ago, a decade ago. See what made you happy. Observe

in your mind how happy you were. Be joyful at what you see. When you've watched the scene long enough, come back to the present, carrying the happiness with you.

3. Another device that can work to give you the feeling of freedom is to imagine yourself skating on a vast body of water. Increase your speed until everything becomes a blur around you and finally disappears in a transparent blending of color. You're free now of all restraints of time and the physical. You can travel into the furthest reaches of your mind.

Because you become caught up in the fantasies, your sense of self-awareness often disappears until you actually seem to be living the fantasy. The energy and sense of exhilaration you find can then carry over to your acting. You borrow from the fantasy to provide energy for the reality. Be aware all the while how creative you are and how creative you want to be and work toward your goal.

NOTES

1. McKim, *Visual Thinking*, 33.
2. Willis Harman, Ph.D., and Howard Rheingold, *Higher Creativity, Liberating the Unconscious for Breakthrough Insights*, (New York: Lothrop Lee & Shepherd Books, 1971), 82.
3. Bill Downey, *Right Brain...Write On!* (Englewood Cliffs, New Jersey: Prentice-Hall, 1983), 5.

Freeing the
Imagination

IMAGINATION IS THAT FACET of ourselves that allows us
to create. It is the catalytic agent, the channel, the conductor to creativity. Without imagination—the power to
see differences, to dream of things outside the realm of
physical existence—we would be little more than robots.

According to Robert Lewis, imagination "allows the
actor to believe what might otherwise be unbelievable. It
helps you to create. It is, therefore, not something mystical,
but a practical tool of your craft." He goes on to say that
the creative actor takes what there is and, using imagination, "makes the part his own creation." The artist makes
the role "more than 'just like life.'" He sees "beyond the
facts, beyond what is there, beyond what others see."[1]

There are many theories about the mind and how it
works, but little is actually known or can yet be proven.
How and why are we able to imagine, to invent, to create?
Nobody knows for certain. But what we do know is that
the "imagination is the instrument of discovery, of casting
light, of shaping psychic concepts of that which is not readi-
ly visible to the conscious senses."[2]

Imagination opens whole realms that otherwise are hidden from us. Not only do we feel joy from our own acts of

HMS Pinafore, directed by Jim Bob Stephenson at Kent State University.

creation, but we can share others' perceptions as well.
Through an imaginative piece of nonrealistic sculpture, we
can discover an artist's reality. Through an actor's interpretation of a role, we can view a unique conception of
truth.

Many experts on creativity emphasize the playfulness inherent in the creative process. It comes from the sense of
freedom that creating brings. When we create, we are like
children who can do as they please, within certain boundaries. Just as children have a sense of freedom from mundane responsibilities, so too does the creative artist. Or at
any rate, the responsibilities are different, more acceptable,
less rigid. Most often an artist is responsible largely to self.
He or she does not have to perform a task in a particular
way. There are no bosses besides self.

Workers on an assembly line have to do things precisely
according to a prescribed standard to please their super-
visors and keep their jobs. There is little room for explora-
tion or creativity. The artist, on the other hand, can
develop an end product from a multitude of processes and
variations. In a different sense, of course, the painter has
to please a patron or a potential customer. The actor has to
please the director, the producer, and the audience. But
perhaps more important, the artist has to please self, often
the hardest taskmaster of all, demanding more time and effort than would any other employer. At the same time,
when the work actually seems like play or recreation, the
task is easier. Such words as "job" and "work" do not really apply.

There can be a sense of accomplishment and pride in
nearly any task completed, yet the creative endeavor
seems to intensify the feeling. This is in large part due to
the fact that when we create we often are doing what we
want. To be successful, of course, a creator needs dis-

cipline. Yet artists usually are more than willing to assume
that discipline and control if it is important for them to
create.

Anyone who wants to create can do so. But not all of us
are interested in the same media. Even in theatre there
are the designers and directors and playwrights. And although a creative person often has talent and ability to succeed in more than one area, temperament or interest may
make that person unfit for any number of creative tasks.
Creative people have to find their niches.

Interest is an indication of future success, but by no
means an assurance. Many will not become good actors because they lack the talent and ability. Others who have
the potential will fail because they do not have the dedication and drive necessary to succeed. The meaning of
"success" here has little to do with money. It means the effectiveness of performance. Finances often do not enter
into the definition of success because at any given time
there are many more actors than jobs.

Why go on then with the preparation for becoming an
actor? Well, ultimately, you have to answer that for yourself. But if you are serious about it and have the potential
and dedication, you probably have as good a chance as
anyone else of making a living at it—even though that
chance is not great.

The following are to help you "stretch" your mind, to
get out of the rut of unimaginative thinking:

1. For this you need several objects normally found
around the house. Sit in a circle, and one at a time pass the
objects to each person. Every time you receive an object,
pretend that it is something else, something suggested by
its shape or size. Rather than stating what you imagine it
to be, present a pantomime to demonstrate its use. For ex-

ample, a letter opener may be come a conductor's baton, a dagger, and so on. A Walkman- type radio may be a Star Trek teleporting device, a notepad, a book, a candy bar, or a building block. Make it plausible; the letter opener could not, for instance, be a broadsword or a machete because it is too small.

2. Imagine yourself an animal. Move in a characteristic yet non- stereotypical way that illustrates the animal. Try to communicate to the rest of the class exactly what you are without saying so in words.

3. Choose a partner. Plan a "scene" in which both of you convey to the class who and where you are, merely by the use of movement and a one- to three-word greeting.

4. Have a classmate place you in a particular pose. Now figure out a logical reason for the pose and follow through with a movement that will communicate exactly what you are doing. Make sure the pose is an important and integral part of the movement. Now assume the same pose and carry through a different set of actions.

5. This is similar to the last exercise. Because the mind tends to make sense out of the nonsensical or the unmeaning, this is a good exercise to try in a number of variations. Have a classmate place you in two separate poses. Now logically go from one to the other, communicating an everyday or commonplace type of activity.

It's a good idea to keep on doing exercises to stimulate the imagination so you will not be thrown by any type of situation or any character you are asked to portray.

Establishing A Proper Frame of Mind

"If we concentrate almost exclusively on our liabilities, then we will establish an almost insurmountable block to achieving our potential."[3] Certainly, be aware of liabilities and learn to compensate for them, but don't dwell on them. Otherwise, they will hold you back.

BELIEVING IN SELF

Of great importance in establishing a framework in which to create is a belief in our worth as creative artists. One way of learning to believe in self is to make an honest list of strengths and weaknesses. For instance, many acting students are told that in today's theatre the person who can sing and dance has the better chance of getting a job. This is true because these talents open up more possibilities. But if you are the type of person who cannot stay on key, you have to accept the fact and go on from there. It doesn't mean that you are worthless. In all probability you have talents that many singers do not.

Again, anyone can be creative, so you must believe that you too can be. And the more strongly you believe, the more likely it is that you will be.

HAVING SENSITIVITY

You can more easily create if you have a deep awareness of the world around you. Sensitivity requires that we get outside ourselves and see things from a variety of viewpoints. Paradoxically, we also must examine our thoughts and feelings and perceptions more deeply. We need to analyze how we feel and why we feel that way.

Sometimes the word "sensitive" applied to an individual has negative connotations. It can refer to a person who is focused inward to the extent of excluding the feelings of others. Many creative people do seem to be "sensitive" in this way in suffering imaginative hurts and slights. But rather than relating everything to self, the artist should be sensitive in the larger meaning of relating to and being aware of the rest of the world. Sensitivity accounts in large part for an actor's being able to interpret and successfully portray a wide variety of roles.

Not everyone is naturally attuned to life. But sensitivity certainly can be developed, and there are many techniques to help do so. Several are included in the exercises at the end of the chapter.

SETTING REALISTIC GOALS

Part of establishing the proper framework for creativity is setting realistic goals. Success in acting depends on talent, ability, dedication, acceptance of self, and concentration. Therefore, it would be totally unrealistic to set a goal of becoming a professional actor after taking one acting class or appearing in a play or two. Although some people seem to attain instant success, it is rare. And it is rarer still for those with little or no background in theatre to remain successful.

BEING FLEXIBLE

It often comes as a surprise to discover that a well-known comedian can play tragedy or has an excellent singing voice. But it happens frequently. We must learn to be flexible in a number of ways in order to be actors.

As photographer Edward Steichen says, "The lack of freedom that an ideology, a nation, a government can impose on an artist is nothing compared with the limitation he can impose upon himself by saddling himself with preconceived notions about things."[4]

As well as referring to the development of talents, flexibility involves our approach to the task of creating. There is an infinite number of ways to interpret a role or a scene or a play. We should not be bound by one idea but should be open to experimentation. Holding to preconceived ideas is a sure way of failing to grow.

According to Silvano Arieti, a creative artist needs to have "gullibility" or openness. This does not mean that creative people should allow themselves to be taken in with unworkable schemes and techniques, but it does mean they should remain open to new ideas and methods. In the last few years, there have been drastic changes in actor training. And much of the new—from the emphasis on games and improvisation to the total discipline of mind and body advocated by Jerzy Grotowski of the Polish Laboratory Theatre—seems to be workable. The evolution of ideas is one of the most exciting things about theatre, and we must be open to new ideas and experimentation to succeed. Otherwise, we will stagnate.

Actors and other creative artists are intuitive. They trust their feelings in part because feelings are the raw material of their creations. Second, they perhaps know that the powers of the mind do work for all of us even when we are unaware of it. Maybe what we deem to be intuitive really is not but has been worked over and over by our subconscious mind. And so the writer has the story unfold before him as on a stage, or the painter without conscious planning sees a mental image of what a painting will become. We must learn to trust in ourselves and our feelings.

Stimulating Our Creativity

To stimulate the imagination, the creative artist needs leisure in which to develop ideas. Creativity cannot exist within a strict routine or with exhaustive regimentation.

Rarely, if ever, do ideas appear full-blown to the actor or other creative artist. There needs to be a period, a time of incubation, to think about the problem. Much of a rehearsal schedule, for example, is directed toward the development of the production and not to the basics of blocking and learning lines.

We also need time to get away from our work—a break from rehearsal and concentration on character development. We need to do something entirely different for a time, or we are likely to suffer burn-out. Then we can return with restored vigor. Often we can change our viewpoints and see solutions that hadn't even occurred to us.

Throughout their lives, most people have been cautioned against "leaping before looking." They are told repeatedly to exercise caution in expressing thoughts and ideas. This may be a good thing in dealing with other people, but it can inhibit creativity. Many excellent ideas undoubtedly are lost through suppression. To be creative, we should learn not to deny any of our first thoughts. They are often the most honest and the most accurate indicators of our feelings. Because of this it is a good idea to get into the habit of recognizing initial responses to people or situations and then developing them. Most thoughts probably do not involve great ideas or discoveries, but if we constantly edit them almost before they surface, then we are certain to miss some that are important.

It can help to keep an idea file. Not only are many ideas suppressed, but others are totally forgotten. If you have a notepad with you to jot down ideas, you will not lose them.

Many come during the night or just before sleep. One reason could be that natural barriers are relaxed, and you are more open to thoughts that bubble up from the subconscious.

Reading also widely stimulates the imagination by building up a reservoir of ideas that an actor may use years later.

Sensory stimulation can cause us to use our imaginations. A few years ago there was a science fiction novel in which alien beings smelled like freshly-cut grass. The author, using one small sensory detail, built an entire novel. So too the way we react to a sensory stimulation can cause us to imagine, and it is impossible to say where the imagination can lead us. Even if it does not result in the creation of a character, it is good practice.

The greater the detail in which we are able to imagine, the more real our imaginary world becomes. We need to get into the habit of daydreaming more and in greater detail. Undoubtedly, success in many kinds of creative undertakings has been determined to a great extent by the creator's being able to imagine a detailed end result.

Another method of stimulating the imagination is to take already existing ideas and expand them. Something used for one purpose can now be used for another. Or we can combine ideas to form something new. A glove compartment door in a car opens to become a tray for drinks. Creativity often involves looking at old ideas in new ways.

Much of what we use in creating is from our own pasts. One way to be certain of retaining the past is to keep a journal. There also are tricks, such as handling and concentrating on articles we've had for years and which have meaning for us. Often if we just let our thoughts flow freely, we will think of things that have long been buried.

The imagination can be stimulated through the use of hypnagogic imagery, which we experience sometimes just before falling asleep. It occurs in an almost dream-like state, involving sensory images. Most common are images of sight and sound, and all are vivid and clear. Often, the images have to do with something we've done during the day. For instance, if we picked blackberries, in the hypnagogic imagery state we might visualize blackberry bushes.

Often the hypnagogic state involves "dream-like fantasies whose novelty is a source of surprise to its possessor." However, the images "are not faithful memory images; memory is infused with fantasy and idealization." Many artists and other creative people have reported using the images as source material.[5]

You are not limited to those ideas discussed here. Whatever works for you is valuable. It matters not what you use to create, but just that you do so.

Stimulating Creativity in Acting

There are many ways of stimulating the imagination in learning to act. Many of the techniques mentioned in the preceding section can work well, but the following are discussed more specifically in relation to acting.

One is to establish an entire characterization on the basis of a single trait. If you are improvising a character, you may decide that she limps. Then you ask why. You tell yourself it is the result of being struck by a car when she was a teenager. How old is she now? She is forty-five. You continue with the questions. How did the accident affect her? She has become bitter. Why? At the time of the accident she was a promising dancer. In fact, dancing was her

entire life. What did she do? Since she had no other interests, she decided finally to teach dance. Why finally? Because for a time she refused to do anything. She simply lay
in bed and let her mother wait on her. How did this affect
the mother, and what did this mean to the dancer?

You can go on and on until a complete character emer-
ges. In doing so, you find yourself increasingly interested in
the person and feeling as if you know her quite well. You
have a good understanding of a character, just by choosing
a random trait with which to begin.

If you are interpreting a character already established
by a playwright, you might try to discover a trait that
would symbolize your character and perhaps even provide
a key to your interpretation. For instance, if you were playing Mary Tyrone, a character in O'Neill's *Long Day's
Journey Into Night* who is addicted to morphine and living
in a dream world of her own making, you might decide
that a distinctive trait is that she tries never to focus her
eyes on anyone. You discover that when her husband
speaks harshly to her, she is startled and does focus on
him. She now sees the reality that she does not care to experience, and at once retreats into her nonfocused world.
This simple trait could provide the basis for the entire interpretation of her character.

In our observations of others, we can see how they react
to a variety of circumstances and situations, and thus take
a distinctive trait we have observed and use it. We all have
empathized with others in many difference circumstances.
When a friend has a failure of some sort—even though we
have never been in the same kind of situation—we can feel
a certain depth of the emotion the other person feels. We
project self into the circumstances of another.

This sort of thing involves imitation or the mimetic instinct, which serves many useful purposes in our lives.

Mimesis is the imitation of another's behavior, speech, idiosyncrasies. This imitation is so instinctive that it's hard not to do it. "Watch people at a movie get expressions of terror on their faces when one of the screen images is in danger. That's mimesis. Ultimately, taken a bit further with a little educating, experience and a lot of freedom, that's acting."[6]

This need for or basic trait of imitating others helps us acquire much of our learning, from imitating our parents when we are beginning to talk to learning through observation how to shoot a basketball through a hoop. Much of children's play involves imitation—playing space explorer or house. Then as creative adults we imitate life and present it through our art. To a great extent, theatre imitates life and asks the audience to pretend that what they are viewing is life. In turn, the audience identifies with the protagonist and suffers when he or she does and rejoices when he or she experiences joy.

In creating a character it can work well to take a trait of another person and apply it extraneously. For instance, if we are playing Henry in James Goldman's *The Lion in Winter*, we can take the strong sense of greed that Harpagon has in Moliere's *The Miser* and apply it to Henry. How does this change the character? What if instead of greed we took the kind of pride that Oedipus Rex has? Now how does Henry's character differ? And how would this change our interpretation of the role? What if Henry were basically shy? Now how would we interpret him?

The first interpretation might portray Henry as somewhat humorous, in ways almost a ludicrous character, which the play certainly implies at times. Or we might portray him as completely unyielding if he has Oedipus' pride, of which there is also evidence in the script. If he had a streak of shyness, he certainly must have hidden it to get where he is in the play. Therefore we might play him as blustering to overcompensate for the shyness. The latter interpretation could in part be justified because at times he is blustering.

What all this means is that we can look at characters in new ways that can help us discover something previously hidden from us. This is just a starting point. We may then drop the extraneous trait. On the other hand, if we find the trait is a valid part of the characterization and seems to work, we can retain it.

Another technique that may help in understanding and interpreting a character is to do something—such as describing your perception of a room or a building—and later have your character describe it.

You can go further and take a character totally out of context. Then have the person react to the new surroundings. When you see the characters away from their usual environments, you have to determine how they would react. This in turn helps you know them better and develop them further.

A final technique for establishing characters is to visualize them as completely as possible. If you are able to do this, you can mentally place them in a variety of situations—much as a novelist might do—and actually "see" how they would react.

Exercises

1. The purpose of this exercise is to help you see that you are a part of a group, and it need not be threatening to you in any way. You need have no fear about other people's reactions when you create a scene or do an exercise in front of them.

Everyone should become a part of a circle, lying down, legs toward the center and slightly spread. Reach out your arms until you are touching the hands of the person on each side. You are a part of the whole. Without you the circle would be broken. Now it is unending, infinite. Close your eyes and think of the circle and know that it depends on you for its completeness, its encompassing wholeness. Feel the unbroken line, the total support of the other members of the group. How fragile the circle is! How delicate its creation! It gives you strength. You are one with it. Yet you are capable of being your Self and expressing your Self and your uniqueness. Relax and enjoy the strength, the unity, the oneness. And remember your thoughts and feelings and color your remembrance.

2. Do word association with someone else. Begin with a word that you or your partner chooses. When your partner reacts, respond by saying the first word that comes to mind. We are so used to suppressing thoughts and feelings that we often do not recognize that we are doing it. If there is any hesitation on either person's part, it is because the person is editing. The first reaction is immediate. There is no such thing as not being able to think of a response. No matter what word you think of, say it. Do not apologize for any of your reactions. Over and over again, take what opportunity you can to get in touch with yourself. Do not judge yourself harshly. It is normal to be hesitant about giving yourself freedom of response. And, incidentally, it is a good idea to do this exercise repeatedly throughout your actor training, which means always if you are serious about acting. If you continue to do the exercise, you will learn to recognize the hesitancies. Then, if you wish, you can eliminate them.

3. Perform this exercise when you are alone and not likely to be disturbed.

Lie back and close your eyes. Imagine yourself a bird, a free- soaring, boundless bird—powerful, capable of flying forever. You lift into the air, your talons pressed back against your body, your feathers sleek in the wind. Fly over fields of tawny wheat just after a rain. You can smell the freshness, feel the cool breeze. Next you see a fast-rushing stream, the water rolling in white whirlpools. Follow the stream with its moss- covered banks to its source in a snow-capped mountain.

Use all your senses to experience your flight—the sound of rushing water, the sense of motion, the coolness and touch of the air. Go on as long as you like and wherever you like, so long as it is pleasant to do so. Then bring yourself back to earth.

4. This exercise is taken from Robert McKim's *Exercises in Visual Thinking*. In a dark room, close your eyes and "squish" your eyelids together. See the luminous patterns. Do the same thing a second time and try to find pictures in the patterns.

5. Present an object to a classmate and receive an object from someone else. Create a fictional story that centers around the object you received and tell it in two minutes or less to the rest of the class.

6. In front of the class, show that you are either too hot or too cold, but try not to do it in a stereotypical manner.

7. Take yourself on another fantasy trip. Go anywhere you wish: to the center of the sun, into another universe, to an unexplored jungle.

8. With someone else, plan a fantasy trip of three to five minutes. One of you should present the first half to the class, having them go along with you in shared imagination. The other presents the second half. Plan only the outline, not the details, before you begin.

9. Begin keeping an idea file and a journal.

10. Think back over the last two or three days. In that time, with whom did you empathize? To what degree? Why?

11. See your class through the viewpoint of your instructor. How do his/her perceptions differ from yours? What accounts for the difference?

12. After you have been keeping your idea file for a week, write a serious poem or humorous short story based on an entry in it. Share the piece of writing with the class.

13. Write a one-page character sketch of the most interesting person you encountered today. What makes the person particularly interesting?

14. Place a character from a short story or play that you know into another set of circumstances from another story or play. Determine how he or she would react.

15. Eavesdrop on a conversation for a minute or two. Write down what you remember of it. Now in light of what you heard, logically extend the conversation for another two minutes.

16. Develop a character in the same way the dancer was developed earlier in this chapter. Then assume the character and react for two minutes with another student who portrays a character established in the same way. You and the other person may decide ahead of time what subject you will discuss.

17. Along with a partner, create a whole new world. Establish its boundaries, natural laws and civilization. There are no other rules on how to create it. When it is finished, have two of your classmates appear in it and react to it in an improvisational scene that lasts approximately two minutes.

18. Choose a historical figure, such as Elizabeth I of England or Chester A. Arthur. Investigate the person's life. Now present an improvisational scene of two or three

minutes in which you play your character while a classmate plays a character from a different historical period. In the scene explain something of significance to the other person. It should be something from your character's own period, but which is outside the realm of the other character's experience. For example, Benjamin Franklin could try to explain electricity to Christopher Columbus. You may ask as many questions of each other as you like. Now the other person explains something to you.

NOTES

1. Robert Lewis, *Advice to the Players*, (New York: Harper & Row, Publishers, 1980), 33-34.
2. Albert Rothberg, M.D., *The Emerging Goddess: The Creative Process in Art, Science and Other Fields*, (Chicago: University of Chicago Press, 1979), 13.
3. Arthur B. VanGundy, Ph.D., *Training Your Creative Mind*, (Englewood Cliffs, NJ: Prentice-Hall, Inc., 1982), 33.
4. Edward Steichen, "On Photography," *The Creative Mind and Method*, ed. Jack D. Summerfield and Lorlyn Thatcher, (New York: Russell & Russell, Inc., copyright 1960 by University of Texas Press. Reissued in 1964 by Russell & Russell), 56.
5. McKim, *Visual Thinking*, 94.
6. Maxine Klein, *Theatre for the 98%*, (Boston: South End Press, 1978), 84.

Thinking
and Acting

WE CANNOT CREATE FROM NOTHING. We have to have a base of experience and knowledge. The larger and more varied the base, the more we have to draw from. Ideas come from something in our present or past and are usually triggered by something we see, read, or experience. These ideas are then held and developed until they become something new.

Getting the ideas relies upon being open to all sensory stimuli. You need to cultivate a sensitivity to others, to your surroundings, and to yourself. Additionally, you need to be sensitive to the workings of your own mind. When an idea stimulates your imagination, let it take over. The only prerequisite is that you know about your surroundings and the way they work. Unless you know life, you cannot, beyond a limited scope, convincingly portray life as an actor.

We need to develop new ways of looking at the world, fresh perspectives. We cannot, however, develop these fresh perspectives if we always view the familiar in the same way. We sometimes need to forget past attitudes and teachings and suspend judgment. We need to be open to new interpretations and views.

Long Day's Journey Into Night, directed by Bedford Thurman at Kent State University (photo by C. James Gleason).

As Charles Brashers says in *Developing Creativity*, "openness means refusing to accept the status quo, with its pre-digested conceptions. It means approaching everything with a sense of wonder and original perception, seeing everything as if it were the only one of its kind."[1]

A large part of our non-seeing can be attributed to the society in which we grew up. As Harman and Rheingold state: "We only see what our culture tells us to see, only know what our society tells us we can know."[2] But just as we can overcome society's stifling of our creative tendencies, we also can learn to go beyond society's bounds in our observations and perceptions.

Studies have shown that we often tend to believe as our parents did. If they followed a particular religion, we are more likely than not to stay with it. Yet often there seems to be no logical reason for acting and reacting to life as we do.

As Rogers and Hammerstein's song in *South Pacific* states, each of us has to be taught our prejudices. We don't instinctively hate and fear others. Society, or our little corner of society, tells us what we are or are not "supposed to do."

In part because of this carryover of belief and prejudice, we all engage in stereotyping, which isn't always bad. As a "shortcut," it allows us to assume certain things without analyzing them in detail.

For instance, when we hear the word "mother," we probably tend to think of a person who is caring, loving, protective, and unselfish. Mother's Day is celebrated because of this stereotype. We can use stereotyping as the starting point for developing a character. But the audience members probably will assume the stereotypical mother unless we tell them otherwise. And though we all acknowledge that mothers often do not live up to their advance billing, we can still be shocked by such books as *Mommy Dearest*. When we assume erroneously, we often have our illusions shattered. As the punch line states: "Don't confuse me with facts."

To be creative we must learn to see beneath stereotypes and dig out what actually is. If we don't do this, our perceptions will be like everyone else's, and we'll have nothing new to point out to our audiences.

What can we do to begin to see with a fresh perspective? As Dorothea Brande suggests, "It will be worth your while to walk on strange streets, to visit exhibits, to hunt up a movie in a strange part of town in order to give yourself the experience of fresh seeing once or twice a week."[3]

Roleplaying is another way of developing a fresh perspective, not only to examine attitudes but to actually try to see the world as others do. Try to look at everyday events and surroundings through someone else's eyes. Walk or drive down the street, looking at houses and stores as a foreigner, as your grandfather, as a friend, as someone who has never seen apartment buildings or huge shopping malls. Or, if you want to portray a character in a play, try to see how this person would view things. What seems different to you now through his or her eyes? In what way?

You often can use what you observe in the present to call up the past. You hear a snatch of an old song that brings back memories. Or the look on a stranger's face reminds you of a long-ago friend. In the System of acting developed by Stanislavski, there is a technique called emotional memory. Simply, this means relating an emotion you felt in real life to the emotion of the character you're portraying in a scene. The idea is to "be" rather than to act or pretend. Yet out of context, it's impossible to recall an emotion and remember exactly how it felt. You must re-

late the emotion to a specific incident, remembering all of
the details. Only then do you begin to feel the emotion.
You take what you feel and apply it to the scene.

Experiment with the concept. Think, for instance, of a
time you were very happy. Where were you? Perhaps it
was your living room. Visualize that room. Remember step-
by-step what occurred. Then relate the feelings and reactions to those that a character in a play is experiencing.
Remember your actions. Alter them to fit your character.

People don't really kick the cat very often or pound
their heads against brick walls. They don't really pace constantly when they're nervous. If they perform these actions at all, they intersperse them with others. Reactions
differ with the people and with the degree of the emotion.

Put yourself in your character's place and really feel as
the fictional person does. Observe others. How do they
react to anger differently than you do? You need to do
more than just gloss over the surface if you want to create
believable characters. You must see all the parts to create a
believable whole.

There is a danger in using emotional memory, though
your own experiences should help you guard against it. It
has erroneously been said that emotional memory is an entirely effective device because once the curtain comes down
each night, the actor who has evoked a particular emotion
can forget it until he or she needs to recall it for the next
performance. Unfortunately, this is not the case. If the
emotion recalled is a strong one that affects you negatively,
you can't just put it aside once you finish a performance.
Because of this possibility, you should weigh whether or
not to recall and reexperience an emotion in detail. Only
you can judge.

Fortunately, you usually do not have to rely on this device. Our memories most often serve us without such an effort if we are sensitive to our pasts.

Sometimes actors confuse emotional memory with sense memory, also practiced by Method (based on the System) actors. Sense memory refers to developing a more complete awareness of what is happening around us. As Emily states in Thornton Wilder's *Our Town*, we need to be aware, to pay attention. So much of life passes us by without our even attempting to catch and hold it. We need to see, touch, taste, smell, hear. When we do so, we experience in both a logical or intellectual way and in a sensory way.

In acting, effective use of sense memory can actively contribute to the audience's willing suspension of disbelief. For instance, properties and set dressings often aren't the real objects but are inexpensive or more logical substitutions. Yet, if you've felt expensive velvet, you can use your sense memory of it to convey its truth to an audience when you are actually feeling a cheaper, coarse fabric. The audience, through you, can revel in the sunlight or smell the ocean breeze.

As Lewis says, "Moods, and yes, emotions can be enhanced by sensory recall."[4] We can use a combination of sense and emotional memory to help build a scene by remembering how something felt or tasted and then how this affected us emotionally. Once we have both memories, we can relate them to the scene in a play, building and intensifying when necessary.

We remember feeling the cold, and we concentrate on each separate sensation: how our toes felt like pegs of wood, how the air seared our throats and lungs and was expelled in puffs like an old steam locomotive, and so on. How did we feel emotionally? Did the cold make us panic

because we were far from home? From this, what can we
relate to a scene where the heat goes off in the house of the
character we're playing? How can we relate this to emotional coldness on our or another character's part?

To develop our sense memories, we need to concentrate
and observe the ordinary. The next time you want to eat
an orange, weigh it in your hand, feel its texture—the
outer skin, the inside sections, the meat. Inhale its odor,
the odor of the skin and the odor of the juice. Taste it; observe the differences in coloration. Learn to do this with
various activities in which you participate—taking a
shower, brushing your teeth, walking outside just after a
rain.

Substituting one sense for another is an excellent exercise to make you think about what you are experiencing.
Hear crimson. How does it sound? What does it communicate to your ear? Or taste the music of Mozart. How does it
differ from that of the Beatles? Or Willie Nelson? Take a
particular theme or selection. Be exact in how it affects the
tastebuds.

Another sensitivity exercise, used in both acting and
psychotherapy, is to block out one sense to concentrate
more fully on another. Use a blindfold and rely only on
hearing. Then add earplugs and rely only on touch.

As Julie Harris says, we need to zero in. "An aerial
photograph of a flooded area doesn't have nearly the impact on a magazine reader as a close-up photograph of a
woman weeping over her destroyed home. What moves us
is not so much events in themselves, but the impact these
events have on human beings with whom we can identify."[5]

It doesn't mean a great deal to us emotionally to hear
that more than one thousand people were killed in an
earthquake. We won't like to read that sort of thing, and

intellectually we will know it's "bad." But only if we can identify with one or more of the people will the reality of what has happened play on our senses. Thus in stories of disasters, a feature writer may do a close-up on one person or one family involved. Up to a point, the more detail we know about the person and the situation, the more fully we can empathize.

How can we learn detail? Part of it, of course, can come through role-playing and through observation. But we need to analyze behavior. We need to figure out the "why" of things. Often, the more we know, the easier it is to figure out motive. Most actors aren't psychologists. Yet they have observed and filed and questioned.

Anything you do that makes you more aware is bound to be helpful in your acting. The following exercises should help. After you try them, you probably will be able to devise additional exercises that are just as effective.

1. Gear yourself to look for ideas. To this end carry a notepad with you. During the first week, try to come up with at least two ideas a day, ideas that could provide the basis for a characterization. Don't be judgmental. When an idea comes to you, jot it down. Don't try to decide then if it's good or not or even whether you want to work with it. Instead, this should be a free association kind of thing with the purpose of teaching yourself to be aware.

2. Get into the habit of looking through the newspaper each day for human interest stories from which you can develop characterizations or build traits to use in portraying other characters.

3. It has sometimes been suggested that to be creative we should learn to look at our surroundings as if we were seeing them for the first time. Do just the opposite. Look at people and objects as if you are seeing them for the last

time. Since you'll never see them again, you'll want to
memorize and remember all the detail. Then write an in-
terpretive description of what you've observed. You can do
this in any manner you like: as a straight description and
what you actually thought or as a character doing the ob-
serving.

4. Tear down a stereotype. Find someone who doesn't
fit the pattern you've been led by society or your environment to believe. How does the particular person not fit the
stereotype? Write a character sketch of the person. Do this
with four or five different kinds of stereotypes.

5. Evoke the past in general. Look at an old building, a
book at a rare book dealer's, or an exhibit at a museum.
Pretend the object you observe is new rather than old. Let
your imagination go. What do you feel? What other people
do you see in this "scene?" What are they doing? What is
the environment in general like? Write about one of the
characters you imagined there, trying to recapture your
mood as you journeyed to the past.

6. Evoke your own past. Get into the habit of spending
five minutes each day by searching your memory and
thinking about a specific time. Or look at an object that relates to your past: a photograph, a piece of clothing, a book
you've kept. Remember the circumstances of each. Who
took the photograph? Who is in it? Why was it taken?
What did it mean to you then? What does it mean to you
now?

Write a nostalgia piece from what you discover. Or an
anecdote for your memoirs. Analyze how you feel now
about this piece of history. Why do you feel this way?

Now take one of the things you've recalled and use it as
a starting point for a character you improvise.

7. Use the technique of "emotional memory" to recall a
time you felt:

enraged
disgusted
sad
joyful
elated
blissful
grieved
frustrated
flustered
tense
ecstatic
resentful
miffed

Remember the exact details of the circumstances surrounding the emotion and try to capture the feelings on paper. Develop a scene or episode to match the ones that interest you the most.

Now take the same scene and write it with a character other than yourself experiencing the emotions and the scene.

Change once more what you do. Take the emotion and how it made you react and apply what you discovered to an entirely different character and scene. Suppose you are miffed that someone apparently snubbed you at a party. Take the same reactions and feelings and apply them to a character of the opposite sex who is "put down" in front of friends by a spouse. How does this affect the reactions? Are they in any way different?

Try this with a variety of emotions, changing the characters and situations around however you wish.

8. There are many things you can do to improve your sense memory.

● Peel and eat a peach or an avocado.

(Experience each sensory detail as you do so. Then remember what you experienced and recapture it on paper. Do the same with the following:)

● Standing in front of the building where you live just after a gentle rain.

● Chewing a piece of gum.

● Tasting lemon juice or vinegar.

● Climbing into bed and pulling up the covers.

● Eating a crispy apple.

● Putting on a T-shirt or pullover sweater.

● Drinking hot chocolate or ice-cold lemonade.

● Frying a hamburger.

Now try to recreate one of these situations without using the objects involved. Eat an apple in your imagination, through pantomime. How well do you actually remember the details of what you did? If you find your memory is faulty, pay particular attention the next time you engage in the activity. Then go through it again using imaginary objects.

9. Block out your sense of sight and concentrate on one of your other senses. First, touch. Either close your eyes or blindfold yourself while in familiar surroundings. Begin to run your fingers over the objects near you. Feel the differences in texture, size, weight, density, shape, and temperature. Run your hands over pieces of fabric and notice the contrast. Determine as much about each object as you can before you move on to another. If you find any-

thing that seems unfamiliar, try to figure out what it is before you remove the blindfold or open your eyes.

Feel the different surfaces of wood on door frames, paint or paper on walls, metal file cabinets or whatever else is near you. Feel the objects with various parts of your body. Touch those that can be lifted to your face. Now try the same thing in different parts of your home.

10. Write thumbnail sketches of one or two new people you happen to see each day. Be as accurate as you can in recording your observations.

11. Take what you write for each character sketch, and on the basis of what you observed, build a more complete character. If a person moved slowly, give a reason. Maybe the person was tired, depressed, or discouraged. Now do the same with people you see engaged in conversation. On the basis of your observations, determine the conversation and its relation to their lives.

12. What further ideas do these sketches or episodes provide? Keep a record in your notebook.

You can do any of these exercises first as yourself and then as another person or a character. This also can help broaden perspective.

Many of these exercises were designed to strengthen a specific type of perception such as sight or sound. This is good practice, but too often we have a tendency to use only one sense at a time in our creativity.

NOTES

1. Charles Brashers, *Developing Creativity, An Introduction,* (La Mesa, CA: Associated Creative Writers, 1974), 55.
2. Harman and Rheingold, *Higher Creativity,* 63.
3. Dorothea Brande, *On Becoming a Writer,* (Los Angeles: Jeremy P. Tarcher, Inc., 1981; reprint of the 1934 edition, Harcourt, Brace and Co., New York), 116.

4. Lewis, *Advice*, 44.

5. Julie Harris and Barry Tarskis, *Julie Harris Talks to Young Actors,* (New York: Lothrop Lee & Shepard Books, 1971), 55.

The Stage

IN ORDER TO USE THE STAGE in an effective and imaginative manner, it is necessary to know the layout. There are three general types of stages in use, although there is a great deal of overlapping, and one specific stage may have characteristics of several types.

The Proscenium Theatre

Most likely, the stage on which you will do most of your acting will be the proscenium stage, also referred to as a picture frame stage. This is because it has an arch that frames the acting area, separating it physically from the audience, which sits facing the action, much as one would view a film. With this sort of arrangement, the audience usually is expected to believe that they are viewing the action through an imaginary fourth wall.

There is as well a psychological separation of the audience and actor. Therefore, it is not difficult to convince the audience that what they are viewing is actual life. In other words, the proscenium theatre lends itself to **representational** plays, those that in effect attempt to create the illusion of actual life being lived behind the arch.

The Lion in Winter, designed and directed by Mary Sesak at Heidelberg College (photo by Jeff McIntosh).

In this sort of theatre, the setting can be more realistic than it can be in an arena or thrust stage theatre, because the audience can see interior walls, made of **flats,** and so can assume the interior of a building. Yet in a sense, the action is *less* realistic than in an arena theatre or, to a lesser degree, a thrust stage. This is because the actor at all times must be concerned with being seen and heard in each part of the auditorium. Although actors don't usually play openly to an audience in a proscenium theatre, they have to make sure not to turn their backs, unless there is a deliberate reason, and to project their lines to be heard by everyone.

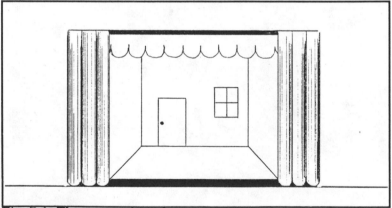

Fig. 5-1: The proscenium theatre.

Even though an attempt is made to convince the audience that they are viewing real life, to do so the spectator must accept many theatrical conventions. The first of these is the movement, which suggests that life outside the theatre is broader in order to be apparent to the last row of the auditorium. It generally is more deliberate and most often is motivated by something in the script. Subtleties of facial expression that communicate a great deal in everyday life are lost beyond the first few rows in a large theatre.

The second theatrical convention the audience is asked to accept is the fact that the two side walls of a set usually slope inward toward the back to provide better sightlines. Furniture is grouped around the three walls, most often leaving a large playing area in the center rather than being scattered around the room as would be found in a real house. Most sets have a much bigger acting area than do their counterparts outside the theatre.

A third and fourth convention are makeup, which is exaggerated so the actors' faces won't "wash out," and lights, which are brighter and more numerous.

Despite all the exaggerations, along with the heightened and more exact dialogue, the audience remains willing to accept the play as life.

How does all this affect the actor? It should become second nature to **dress the stage** to provide a pleasing picture, to **share** with another actor so that both of you are equally **open** to the audience. You should learn the different areas and the terms applied to them, as well as the general **blocking** terms the director will use in staging your movement and **business**. Then you can concentrate more fully on interpreting the character and the play, rather than on technique.

STAGE AREAS

During the Italian Renaissance, when proscenium theatres were first constructed, stages were raked or sloped upward to the rear wall of the theatre. That is why **Upstage** means the area furthest from the audience, while that closest to the audience is **Downstage**. (To "upstage" someone is to force him or her to look upstage

toward you.) **Stage Right** is the area to the actors' right
as they face the audience, and **Stage Left** the actors' left.
Center, of course, is the middle of the acting area. From
these four terms, it is easy to determine where the action is
blocked to take place. **Up Center** is the middle area
toward the back wall and **Down Center** is the center of
the stage closest to the audience. Usually in a script the
names are abbreviated, such as DL (Down Left) or UR
(Up Right).

UR Up Right	UC Up Center	UL Up Left
RC Right Center	C Center	LC Left Center
DR Down Right	DC Down Center	DL Down Left

Fig. 5-2: Areas of the stage.

In most proscenium stages there is an **apron** or
forestage that projects out in front of the proscenium
arch. It can be almost any size. The further out it projects,
the more playing space there is near the audience. Aprons
or forestages are often used for **presentational plays,**
wherein the actor speaks directly to the audience.

The proscenium stage offers several advantages. First,
the scenery can be more realistic, and the curtain can be
closed for scenery shifts. Actors can wait just offstage for
their cues, and scenery and props can be stored close to the
acting area but away from the audience's view.

Those who use a proscenium stage need to be concerned with presenting a pleasing picture in the composition of the setting and the placement of the actors. A disadvantage is that there cannot be the closeness between audience and actor that is desirable for some plays.

Because body position is important in proscenium theatre, it is helpful to know those shown in the following diagram. Most often the major characters in a particular scene would be in one of the positions in the lower half of the circle, that is between profile and full front. Only rarely are the other positions used, except if an actor is not the center of focus or if a certain effect is desired.

Most often two actors of equal importance will remain on the same level between downstage and upstage, although they may face slightly front rather than being in complete profile.

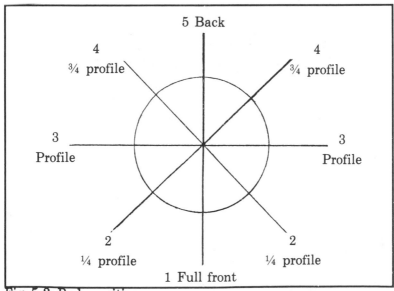

Fig. 5-3: Body positions.

A moving actor will draw more attention, whether going from one spot to another or fiddling with a prop.

There are many other ways of providing focus on an actor or a group of actors.

Strongest is the #1 area. The others decrease in strength the higher the number. In 5-4a, the #2 area is weaker than #9 because the actor is facing upstage. All three actors in 5-4b are of equal strength facing front.

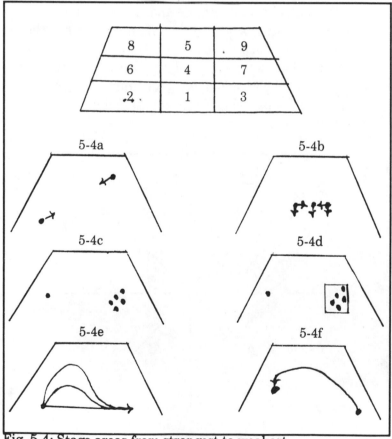

Fig. 5-4: Stage areas from strongest to weakest

When those on the ends face inward, the one in the center
is the point of focus. In 5-4c, the isolated individual receives
the emphasis, while in 5-4d the emphasis is just about
equal when the group is on a platform. The movement
that is the strongest, 5-4e, is the straight line. The others
show decreasing strength or uncertainty. In 5-4f, however,
we see that moving in a curved line is stronger than
moving in a straight line because of final positioning. If the
actor walked toward the back wall, he or she would be
facing upstage, a weak position.

The Arena Theatre

Neither the body positions nor the terms describing acting areas in the proscenium theatre mean anything in
arena theatre. Nearly everything is different.

In the arena theatre, the audience surrounds the action.
The acting area, with historical precedent in the theatres
of ancient Greece, usually is square or oval. Whereas in
proscenium theatre the stage is usually raised above the
audience, in arena theatre the acting area is lower. The
seats are raked downward from the outer walls of the
theatre toward the stage.

Since the audience surrounds the action, there must be
a different way to describe the acting space. A common
practice is to designate areas to correspond to the dial of a
clock. One area is the twelve o'clock position, another
three o'clock and so on. Another way is to name the areas
after geographical directions.

There is nothing to physically separate the audience and
the actor, which thus provides a greater sense of intimacy.
For the actor this means there can be more subtleties of facial expression and movement than in a theatre where the

audience is seated a great distance from the playing area.
An actor who wants to communicate directly to the
audience can do much better with arena staging than with
proscenium. The nearness also allows the audience members to feel involved.

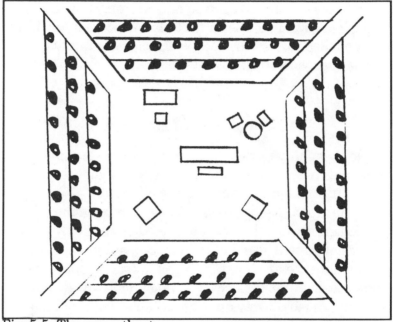

Fig. 5-5: The arena theatre.

The major disadvantage is that it is difficult to conceal
anything. Actors cannot wait offstage but may have to
make longer entrances and exits, and properties not in use
either have to be stored in sight of the audience or have to
be carried through the aisleways to the acting area. Because the audience surrounds the action, arena theatre has
many requirements of setting not found in proscenium
staging. There can be no realistic sets with walls, although

transparent cloths, called **scrims**, are sometimes used to suggest the appearance of walls.

The properties have to be more realistic since the audience sits closer to the action and can spot substitutes. The furniture has to be low enough for audience members to be able to see over.

The actor or director cannot be so much concerned with presenting a pleasing picture, since what would be aesthetically pleasing to one area of the audience may not be to another. A bigger concern is to make sure that all of the audience will be able to see at least most of the action. There are no weak areas now as there could be in proscenium theatre. The only exception is center stage because only half the audience can see the face of an actor who stands there. If the actor plays off center but faces toward center, he or she is showing a portion of the face to more than half the audience. An actor in an aisleway or corner can, just by turning the head, face all the audience. There can be greater variety in playing areas since the groupings are more plastic and moveable. However, body position doesn't mean much. An actor who is open to one part of the audience is closed to another. Similarly, upstage for some viewers is downstage for others.

There are different considerations in the matter of focus. Instead of placing an actor upstage and having the other actors play to him to provide a focal point, the actor in an arena theatre relies on such devices as standing while others sit or moving while others are motionless. Overall, the actor in an arena theatre has to pay more attention to subtleties of characterization that would be lost in a large proscenium theatre.

In proscenium theatre, groupings can be important. In the following, for instance, the actor alone would probably be the center of attention, or the two groups could suggest a conflict with each other. But in arena theatre, spacing is unimportant; an actor who appears separate from the group from one part of the audience appears to be part of it at another.

In proscenium theatre, body positions can tell the audience a great deal. Those in weak areas such as UR or UL often appear to be hidden in a corner. But in arena theatre, body positions relate to the other actors and not to the audience. In proscenium theatre distance can convey psychological implications, which it cannot in arena theatre. However, an actor can move away or come closer to the other actors on an arena stage and give a sense of psychological closeness or separation through the movement.

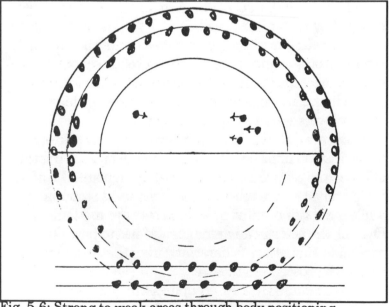

Fig. 5-6: Strong to weak areas through body positioning.

By keeping at least four feet of space between each
other, the actors will open the scenes for all parts of the
audience. If two actors face each other directly at close
range, each one's back is to part of the house, at the same
time blocking the other actor from the same part. It is better if each stands slightly sideways in relation to the other.
Most positions are not bad if they are held only briefly.

In two-character scenes, one or both actors can stand
near an aisleway, providing better sightlines. Often, since
the actor speaking cannot be the center of attention for the
entire audience, reactions through facial expression and
movement become more important. With three characters
there can be a triangle so that most viewers will be able to
see one actor full front and another in profile.

The Thrust Stage

The third type of theatre is the thrust stage, which con-
tains a playing area similar to that of the arena theatre except that one side opens into a stagehouse or back wall.
The audience sits around the three remaining sides. Most
often the stage is lower than the audience.

Since there is a back wall, more scenery can be used
than in arena theatre but not as much as on a proscenium
stage. **Box sets** cannot be used, but at least there can be a
background for the actors. As in arena theatre, the
audience is closer to the actor, and there is no physical
separation such as there is in the proscenium arch.

More intimacy is possible than in proscenium theatre.
But again, more realistic properties must be used.

There are various other stages, but they are simply
modifications of these three. Some have a proscenium
stage with a large apron or forestage that extends out

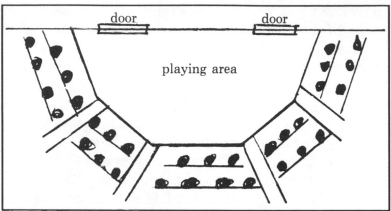

Fig. 5-7: The thrust stage.

toward the audience in front of the proscenium arch. Some platform stages are built without framing devices, and some theatres have ramps extending into the audience. Some have side stages, small acting areas outside the proscenium arch and on either side of the main stage.

A great deal of difference exists among theatres of a particular type. Some proscenium theatres seat few spectators while others seat hundreds. Of course, intimate plays would be less effective in a large theatre, and elaborate productions would suffer in a theatre that seats less than a hundred.

The Body

OUR BODIES ARE CONSTANTLY communicating our thoughts and feelings. We communicate much more nonverbally than with the use of words. So it is extremely important that we treat our bodies for what they are: the major tool through which we communicate as actors. Through work and training we need to make our bodies as expressive as we can.

How do we communicate with our bodies? Through facial expression, posture and carriage, gestures, touching, and spatial distances. You can reveal your personality, show how you are feeling at a particular moment, and convey whether or not you are verbally telling the truth.

Just as we learn to speak by imitating, we learn as infants and children what certain nonverbal signs convey. Even knowing these signs, we still often give ourselves away by broadcasting feelings that we would just as soon others did not pick up.

Overall, we have learned what certain gestures—such as nodding and shrugging—mean. But there are many other behaviors we need to be aware of as actors. These behaviors often give more "meat" to a characterization than do words. Certainly they would if we were playing the mute female lead in Mark Medhoff's *Children of a Lesser God*. But more than that, think, for instance, of how Willy

Long Day's Journey Into Night, directed by Bedford Thurman at
Kent State University (photo by C. James Gleason).

Loman in Arthur Miller's *Death of a Salesman* would
project his feelings of defeat and hopelessness by slumping
his shoulders and dragging his feet. Immediately, this sets
the tone of the play.

Communicating As Character And As Self

An actor's body communicates another whole range of
ideas because the performer is both self and a character.
Moreover, self and character communicate both to the
audience and to the other actors. This means that when
we act, we have to be certain all these different aspects
mesh, that we stay "in character" and still communicate
both as character and as skilled performer.

It is the actor's job to take only that which is desirable of
self and can co-exist logically with a character and transmit it to an audience. Certainly, this is an enormous under-
taking and so should be considered only an ideal. Yet, "the
show must go on."

What does that mean? It means simply that we cannot
as actors let our personal lives interfere with a performance. Of course, we will transmit any severe physical condition that is a part of us rather than the character. But we
can try to integrate it with the character, make it as much
a part of the role we are playing as possible. In *Children of
a Lesser God*, it has been traditional to cast deaf or partial-
ly hearing people in corresponding roles, making a physical condition work for instead of against the performance.

What we can and should filter out of a performance are
minor aches and pains and minor and/or temporary
problems and worries. Many an actor has held a sneeze or
cough till after the curtain closes.

We have to try to make positive those parts of ourselves that we present to the audience. To fellow performers who may be aware of our true selves, we need to project the confidence that no matter what the "outside noise" affecting us, we can succeed in playing our roles to the best of our abilities.

It is our job as actors to determine our character's physical traits, liabilities, habits and so on. These characteristics have to be consistent with what the playwright has written and consistent from the beginning of the play to the end. The actor's body has to be trained enough or responsible enough to be able to portray a variety of physical characteristics and make them believable. If we play the lead in Bernard Pomerance's *The Elephant Man*, we have to convince the audience we are suffering great physical deformity, even though in fact the grotesqueness is only projected with the imagination, not through the use of makeup or costuming.

We have to be aware enough and attuned enough to our bodies to be able to have them communicate onstage what we wish. Certainly, we cannot always be completely aware of everything we are communicating, but we have to have at our command expressive, subtle ways of projecting meaning and thoughts.

When certain performers appear before an audience, the air seems almost to sparkle with the electric quality they generate, while others, who technically may be every bit as good, do not seem to come as much alive. Admittedly, there is a bit of mystery here that defies analysis. Yet, we can to a degree dissect an electrifying performance. It has several identifiable qualities. First is the actors' ability and desire to concentrate. Behind electrifying performances we can sense the actors' total involvement in the performance. They are "up" for the presentation, involved and attentive not to self but to the entire theatrical experience. They are attuned second by second to what is occurring in the playing area and auditorium.

Next, this type of performer is joyful in the creation. Even though the joy is outside the role itself, it is communicated to the audience and to the other performers through an actor's command of his or her performance and by no means interferes with the mood of the play itself. It exists in the exclusion of outside noises or concerns, almost denying existence beyond the creation of the art form itself. This sort of thing occurs only if we transcend personal concerns. The overly nervous actor, thinking of how well he or she will do, is neither projecting self nor the role to the best advantage.

The third quality of an electrifying performance is confidence. The person with the greatest stage presence never doubts that he or she will be able to transmit the truthfulness of the role, the play, and the production. When we see such a performer, we feel almost drawn in as by a powerful magnet. At the same time, the actor seems nearly to burst through the fourth wall in projecting the integrated personality of self and role to the audience.

Those fortunate enough to appear in a production with such an actor also are buoyed up by the performance. Often they feel drawn up to a higher level of performance themselves, able to transcend their own abilities.

Exercises

1. Lie flat on the floor, arms and legs slightly spread. Now concentrate on each part of your body coming alive. Start with the toes and work your way upward, waiting until you feel a tingling in each part of your anatomy.

2. Choose a partner. One of you assume a facial expression that depicts a particular emotion. The other person

should mirror that emotion and then adapt it to fit his or her own personality. Now switch and do the same thing again.

3. This is similar to Exercise 2. Work in pairs. One of you should try to communicate a feeling or emotion through posture and carriage. The other person then assumes the same bearing and adapts it to fit his or her own personality. Switch and do the same thing.

Body Language

One aspect of body language is **gestures.** There are four types:

1) directive or indicative
2) descriptive or illustrative
3) expressive or emphatic
4) private or self-communicative

The first type is fairly apparent. It includes pointing, beckoning, shaking the head, or waving someone away. Many directive gestures are exact and unvarying, carrying one unmistakable meaning, at least in a particular culture. If you are playing someone from an alien culture, you, of course, need to do some investigating.

The second type of gesture is less exact, though when accompanied with words, is fairly self-apparent. We spread our arms and say, "The fish that got away was this long." We point to our ear and make a circular motion with our hand, then point to someone else, telling them, "You're crazy."

The third type is for emphasis. We throw our hands up in the air in protest. We spread our arms and shrug our shoulders. We pound a speaker's stand with the side of our fist. Certainly, these are fairly accurate manifestations of a feeling or state of mind. But without words it is difficult to tell what they relate to.

The last type is meant only for self, although the gesture may be the exact same one we use to communicate to someone else. We tap a foot on the floor or a pencil on the edge of a desk. We grimace or purse our lips. All of this is done in reaction to something in our environment, in these cases something that displeases us, although these gestures can be done for a wide variety of reasons. Often we aren't even aware we're doing them.

All these things can add greatly to or strengthen our characterizations. But they have to fit the personality and the circumstance.

Besides this, there are other considerations when using gestures in any type of performance. Probably the most important consideration is whether the gestures are natural, not only to our character but to us as well. There's nothing that communicates being ill at ease so much as inhibited or self- conscious gestures.

For some reason, speakers, actors, or singers often begin to worry about their hands, when in everyday life they think of them very little. They tend to make tiny gestures that can barely be seen and rarely rise above the level of the waist. They call attention to themselves because of their self-conscious aspect. They communicate much more about the actor than about the role and so detract from the performance.

A gesture has to fit the actor/character, the situation in the play, and the size of the audience. For a lucky few, even when first beginning to act, the use of gestures is almost second nature. These people automatically adjust the expansiveness to fit the size of the audience. But many actors, at least at first, are more inhibited.

The gesture should grow out of the role itself and in the character's relationship with others. Only when you have confidence should you even begin to think about them, unless they are an integral part of the plot. The best advice is: Don't worry about gestures and in all probability you will gradually begin to feel comfortable with them.

A second type of body language is **carriage and posture.** We all can tell, for instance, that a person who sits with feet under a chair, shoulders rounded, and arms clasped in front of the chest in all probability is not open to conversation or interruption of any kind from the outside world. Unless we know more about the situation, we cannot deduce exactly what the body language is saying, except that it is negative. It could mean the person is feeling depressed, inadequate, ashamed, or guilty.

On the other hand, if someone were sitting in the chair, legs stretched out in front, trunk leaning back, hands hanging at the sides or hooked into pants' pockets, we would infer openness and expansiveness.

Hundreds of positions and carriages are easy to understand, at least in a broad sense, and there have been dozens of studies made of various physical behaviors. Important to remember is that this sort of thing can certainly enhance a role, once you figure out what would be characteristic overall and likely in the changing circumstances of the script.

The third type of body language is **movement,** either while standing in place or in going from one spot to another. We convey nervousness, for instance, by pulling at a button, constantly smoothing back our hair, or biting a lower lip. We communicate happiness by a springy step, rising high on our toes as we walk across a room.

Exercises

1. Try to communicate a particular mood or feeling to the rest of the class through the use of gestures.

2. Do the same thing through carriage or by moving from one spot to another.

3. Now use all three types of movement—gesture, position and carriage, and movement—to develop a scene or story to present to the class. Present it only nonverbally. It should be at least a minute in length and should have a definite beginning, middle, and end.

4. Portray a type or a character other than yourself through the use of movement. Try to do it well enough so that the rest of the class can figure out the situation and the character type. Do this nonverbally and without props.

Freeing the Body

To use the body effectively, you should do your best to keep it in good condition.

Many actors take specialized classes in such areas as fencing, dancing, or martial arts, which certainly are an advantage in keeping in good physical shape and also increasing the variety of roles a person can play. But with or without the classes, anyone serious about acting needs to follow a regular regimen of exercise.

Aerobic exercises are best overall for keeping the body toned. These include walking, jogging, running, swimming, and bicycling. (Other exercises are fine but will not have the overall, general benefit. Also, check with your physician before starting a serious exercise program. A number of books are available on the subject, too.)

You need to keep yourself physically centered. This refers to having the proper alignment or posture for you, the individual.

Unfortunately, the majority of us have sloppy postures. But when we are centered, our chins are parallel with the floor, shoulders both at the same level, the spine straight, the arms hanging straight from the shoulders, the knees relaxed, the abdomen firm, and the buttocks tucked in. Once you get used to this posture, you will see that you feel relaxed. You can project yourself well on the stage and in everyday life. Of course, you will vary the position if necessary for whatever role you play.

To be sure your body is free of tension, continue the relaxation exercises you learned in Chapter 2. Vary them with new exercises of your own devising.

Filling Space

The way you come across as an actor depends to a degree on your posture and carriage, in other words how you fill space.

You alter the plasticity of your environment by how you move and how you appear in a fixed position. You are an element in a kind of sculpture, comprised of everyone and everything within your immediate presence.

The setting, the stage, and the seating areas are altered each time you change your spatial relationship with any part of that overall sculpture. The better, the more appropriately, you fill and alter the space around you, the more effective the overall production. Appropriateness is tied in with the total ensemble, the mood and theme of the play and the characterization.

As you learned, in a proscenium theatre, the director
and actors must be concerned with presenting an aesthetically pleasing picture. This does not necessarily mean a
symmetrically balanced stage. Rather it should be one that
shows the "beauty" of the play. "Beauty" in this sense
does not necessarily mean having faultless lines and per-
fectly harmonious colors. Rather it presents the truth of
the drama itself. It in some way depicts or emphasizes the
theme or characterization or situation. It is fitting to the
particular unfolding of the production.

What might be theatrically effective for a given scene
might otherwise be considered ugly. However, if it points
up or complements the action of the play, then it is effective. A great deal of this, then, has to do not only with color
and "beautiful" and line but psychological and emotional
implications.

To be part of this aesthetically pleasing presentation, we
need to learn to fill space effectively as individuals; only
then can we best apply what we know to our characterization. If we stand alone in opposition to the other characters
in a play, we fill a slightly different part of space. Yet by
our carriage and movements, we fill it appropriately. Our
particular globe of space might be much smaller or larger
than another character's, depending on the type of person
we are portraying. Yet we need to fill space not always
with the gracefulness of a dancer, for instance, but with
the grace of a character, which actually may portray a kind
of ugliness. But the ugliness, because it is fitting, portrays
truth and thus aesthetic beauty.

Think of your globe of space as a kind of bubble that
most often remains separate from others. This seems to
imply that there are as many bubbles on stage as there are
actors. But this is not always the case with extremely close
relationships.

Much has been written on the matter of territory and territorial rights. At its simplest, it refers to an animal staking out a certain part of a forest as its own. Territorial rights account for the belief that to invade another's house is somewhat akin to physically violating that person. Personal space has a great deal to do with privacy.

We usually do not infringe on the space of strangers; we mind our own business. Each person is entitled to his or her own little bit of space in the classroom, on the street, or even on a crowded bus, though the globe shrinks or expands depending on the situation. But it cannot shrink too far and remain that way, or there will be conflict. Neither can it expand too far, for most of us would not be able to stand the loneliness. Territorial rights, of course, apply to countries as well, and international disputes are often the result of a disagreement on what constitutes a country's territory.

In many foreign cultures, personal space is smaller than in the United States. Americans would feel uncomfortable standing as close in conversation as many people from other cultures stand. Yet even in these countries, it is taboo to go beyond a certain point.

But there are exceptions. The closer emotionally you are to another person, generally the closer you can be physically. There are occasions, between parent and child or between lovers, where the bubbles have melded so closely that it is difficult to see that two actually exist.

Yet most often we are responsible, both as individuals and actors, for our own space. Even in group scenes, with three or more actors occupying a certain portion of the stage, the bubbles or globes would look something like this...

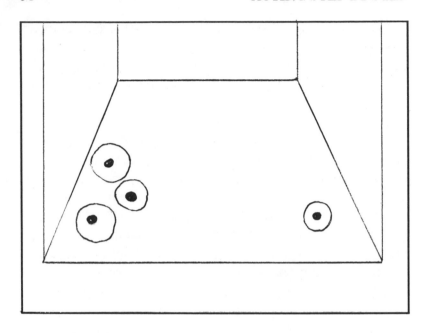

...rather than like this...

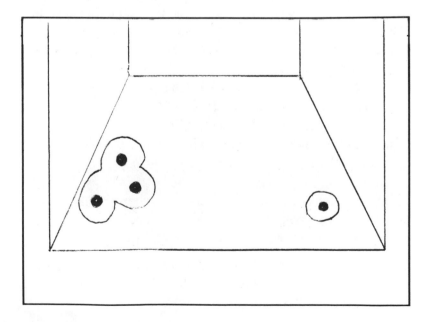

We need to learn best how to fill our own spaces and the portion of space we share with others. A great deal of this depends on the director's interpretation and blocking. Yet the nuances and subtleties are usually the actor's responsibility.

A general rule might be: The more powerful the individual (whether in real life or as a character in a play), the larger the globe. Several years ago there was a big to-do over the fact that one of San Diego's mayoral candidates, while escorting the visiting Queen Elizabeth of England to a speaker's area, reached out and touched her arm to help guide her. This is considered by many English citizens as totally inappropriate because one simply does not invade the space of royalty.

Whether due to cause or effect, the higher the social class, the larger the space. In films or plays, it is easy to note that in a gathering of peasants there is a greater physical closeness than there is among people of a higher social class. Not only is this the case among peers, but those from lower classes keep a greater distance from those in higher classes than they do from each other. Possibly this is because the upper class connotes money and hence greater worth, or maybe it is fear of feeling the effects of power.

Exercises

1. Take the character of Willy Loman in *Death of a Salesman* and visualize the globe of space he might fill. In what way would he fill it? Develop a stance or posture based on this character.

Now take the character of Mark Antony from Shakespeare's *Julius Caesar*. How would the globe differ in size now, and how would you fill it? Develop a stance or posture appropriate to this character.

Do the same with Nora in Ibsen's *A Doll's House*. With
the character of Julie in Strindberg's *Miss Julie*. In the latter Julie is the highborn one, yet she is in a sense at the
mercy of a member of the lower class. How might you thus
visualize her globe or her characteristic way of carrying
herself?

2. Experiment with the matter of territory or personal
space. Step by step, move closer to someone in the class
whom you do not know well. Get as close as you can
without reacting physically. Then analyze when you began
to feel uncomfortable.

This experiment may teach you some valuable lessons
about body language. Even though we do our best to follow through on something like this, our bodies often give
clues that oppose the action. We may stiffen perceptibly,
turn our heads so we are not seeing eye to eye, lean slightly backwards from the person, and so on. Of course, a
character in a play would have similar reactions, at least
those consistent with his or her personality.

Using Space

Physical movement on stage serves a number of purposes. It keeps a play from appearing static; it shows
psychological and emotional relationships; it portrays
character; it points up the emotional content of a scene.
Yet it has to be motivated by the script or at least appear
to be.

The movement and blocking have to fit the type of play.
Actors would not generally rush back and forth during a
presentation of *Macbeth*, nor would they walk majestically
and slowly as Oscar and Felix in Simon's *The Odd Couple*.
Different characters move differently, even within the con-

text of a play. Once you figure out a character's way of walking, you have gone a long way in understanding personality and motivation.

It is important to determine the quality of movement. Even slight differences in posture contribute to the impression you make on others. This is further emphasized when the character moves.

There are two categories of movement and business in a play: **inherent** and **supplementary**. Inherent business is any action that advances the story or is an integral part of the plot. It includes exits and entrances, fights and phone calls. Supplementary business is added for effect, either to enhance the message of the play or to establish character. It includes how the actor stands, sits, or walks. This business helps to establish the mood of each scene and the emotions of the characters.

As mentioned, physical closeness sometimes implies emotional closeness, whereas distance often implies disagreement. A tendency to stay in certain areas of the stage can show much about the psychological aspects of a character. One who stays toward the back of the set probably seems timid, whereas another who is downstage appears more extroverted or confident. A scene appears weak if the characters constantly move behind the furniture rather than in front. A dominant character usually will not stand looking up at a platform while browbeating a weaker character, or the effect is humorous.

Through movement and placement, the audience is aware of conflict, focus, emphasis, and characterization. Movement can complement or even replace lines. It can show the progression of the play or prepare the audience for future events.

There's a theory that when we assume the physical characteristics of an emotion, we soon can begin to feel that emotion. Frown slightly and turn down the corners of your mouth, and you'll begin to feel sad or self-pitying. Crinkle the corners of your eyes and smile, and you'll start to feel happy.

You can take this further. Figure out something characteristic about a person's face or carriage and assume this characteristic. Then you can begin to feel as you imagine the person feels. You can put on the character's personality as you put on the physical characteristics.

We cannot all have the bodies we want. But we can learn to express and create with the bodies we have.

Exercises

1. Create a one-minute situation and the surrounding circumstance to show an emotion: anger, joy, sorrow, disgust, or frustration. Present the scene to the rest of the class.

2. Randomly perform actions for five to ten seconds without planning anything out ahead of time. Now establish a reason for the actions and present a scene showing the reason and incorporating the action into it.

3. Develop an original character as completely as you can or take a character from a well-known novel or play. Figure out how the person is likely to move. Now walk from one side of your classroom or stage to the other, showing as much about the character as you logically and realistically can. Discuss with the rest of the class what was communicated.

4. Move randomly until the movement begins to have meaning. Then continue with the movement showing the meaning to the rest of the class.

5. Watch someone performing a task, such as preparing a particular food, washing his or her hair, or selling a

newspaper. Then, step by step, recreate the movements, leaving nothing out, adding nothing new.

6. Move in the way you think the following people would in these situations:

- a policeman closing in on a dangerous criminal;

- a sailor crossing the deck of a ship;

- a postman carrying a bag of mail in the late afternoon, a day or two before Christmas, or as any other person would be likely to move as part of a job.

Have the class try to figure out the type of person you are portraying.

7. Listen to a recording of music of your choice. When you think you are ready, interpret the music with your body without following any particular pattern of dance steps.

The Voice

A CTING CAN BE JUST AS DEMANDING on the voice as on the body, so we need to learn to speak in a natural way without strain. Of course, we cannot all have deep, mellow voices, but unless there is some physiological cause, we should be able to develop our voices so they can be effective tools for stage use.

Voice Production

The first prerequisite of good vocal production is proper breathing. Even though we have been breathing all our lives, we do not necessarily do it correctly.

Many of us have a tendency to breathe largely with the chest. This shallow type of breathing usually is more than adequate to sustain us through our daily activities, and it is closest to the "proper" type of breathing when we need a quick supply of fresh oxygen while running or jogging. For acting we need to breathe in a different way, to have better control of the air passing in and out of our lungs. Often in speech or voice classes, the student is asked to sustain an exhalation of breath for as long as possible, holding a particular note.

Paul Green's *Trumpet in the Land*, directed by Charles Kray. The show is presented each summer season in a large outdoor amphitheatre where voice control and projection are of major importance.

If done correctly, this is a good exercise to determine if you are using the breathing mechanism to the best advantage. Many people cannot seem to control exhalation for longer than ten or fifteen seconds. This tells them they need to work on developing proper breathing. But the exercise also works against itself. There is often a tendency to speak or sing "from the throat," rather than from the lungs, when we are running out of air. Thus we are straining and risk losing our voices.

To produce sound, the vocal folds vibrate when a column of air passes through them. It's a fairly automatic process; the vocal folds adjust as we want them to. Yet if we attempt to project our voices without breathing properly, we tense our throats; we try to "squeeze" out the sound.

To relax the tension in the throat, let your jaw drop open. Produce an "ahhh" without trying to focus or project, and don't worry about how you sound. Pay attention to how you feel, then try to carry the relaxed feeling over to other voiced sounds. Relaxed humming also is good. You should not have to force if you learn to breathe correctly.

What is proper breathing for speech? Generally, it is the way we breathe when we are lying down. We take in larger quantities of air, filling the abdomen and the chest, inhaling and exhaling an unobstructed flow of air.

To learn to breathe in this way, try lying on your back. Push as hard as you can against your abdomen with the palms of your hands. Suddenly release the abdomen, and the air should flow in. Now try the same thing standing up. Keep trying till it becomes second nature to breathe deeply when you speak or sing.

The more that is required in the way of vocal projection, the more control you need to have of your breathing. In a 100-seat theatre you will not need the capacity or breath control you will in a 1,500-seat amphitheatre. For an easy-going character who experiences no highs nor lows of emotion, you will not need the breath control you will for an emotional role or scene. Yet to be able to play a variety of roles, you should be certain you have the capacity for doing what is demanded without damage.

One of the best aids to good voice production and projection is good posture, which supports your vocal mechanism and gives it room to operate in an effective manner.

You need to use your resonators to their best advantage. Resonators are those parts of the body that provide amplification for the voice, such as the tubing of a brass instrument or the sounding board of a piano. They include the throat, nose, and mouth, as well as the bones in the head and the chest. Their purpose is to enrich and reinforce the original tone.

The more relaxed the throat, the more pleasant and full the resonation. Tension may cause undesirable voice qualities, such as whininess or breathiness. Speaking at at improper pitch also affects resonation and can tire or damage the voice.

To determine if you are speaking at the proper pitch level, use a piano to assist in seeing how high and how low you can sing comfortably without strain. Some people, of course, will have much broader ranges than others. This doesn't really matter as far as speaking is concerned.

Count how many notes in your range and divide by four. A fourth of the way from the bottom should be your "habitual pitch." This means the note you hit most often in speaking. To see if that is the case, simply start to talk and sustain one of the notes rather than cutting it off. Certainly, you will not always hit the same note, nor should you try. You should be speaking within the range of this particular note, higher or lower depending on such factors as emotional content or situation.

Just as the body needs to be relaxed and warmed up, so does the voice. Many of the relaxation exercises you learned earlier help with preparing the voice for performance. A few others follow. But remember, when using your voice, always keep something in reserve. If you don't, you risk tiring yourself and straining without realizing it.

Exercises

1. Stretch the jaw as much as you can, pulling it from side to side.

2. Yawn two or three times to open up the throat.

3. Exhale as sharply as you can and then let the air rush back in.

4. Forcefully project the following lines against the far wall of your classroom or theatre, visualizing the sound waves breaking it down:

a. "I'll huff and I'll puff and I'll blow your wall down."

b. "Open up in the name of the law."

c. "If you don't come out right now, I'm coming in to get you."

d. "Your house is on fire; you'll have to jump."

Articulation

Another aspect of voice usage is articulation, the forming of consonants using the lips, teeth, tongue, alveolar ridge, hard and soft palates, and glottis. The way these are positioned, as far as contact or near contact with one another, determines the particular sound. Slight differences account for regional dialects or accents. Vast differences, whether physiological or out of habit, result in unintelligible speech.

You should learn to speak clearly without emphasizing the sound so much that it calls attention to itself.

Nothing sounds worse than for the character in a play to have a regional accent that is not consistent with his or her background. The generally accepted "dialect" in the United States is called mid-American standard and is pretty typical of the midwest, without the twang. Nearly all newscasters speak in the generally accepted way. If you are not sure of your own speech, try tuning into the evening news and matching the speech patterns to your own.

Typically, Americans have sloppy speech habits. This means they are lazy about proper articulation. It's easier to pronounce a "d," rather than a "t," in words such as "better," or to say "probly" instead of "probably." It's easier to say "tick" for "thick" or "dis" for "this."

In class, try reading aloud speeches from a number of plays. Have your instructor and your classmates try to determine any distortions or omissions. If any are found, work on trying to correct them.

Voice Usage

Voice and speech are secondary functions of the vocal mechanism, which is primarily associated with breathing and eating. These are absolutely necessary for survival, whereas we could survive without speech, though it would probably be a very dull world.

The sounds we make with our vocal mechanisms can, so far as we know, be more exact and varied than those of other life forms. Even so, we make many nonverbal sounds, those that can communicate though not through

the symbols we call words. We cry, wail, hum, grunt, or
scream, and the variety within each of these types of
sounds can have any number of meanings, from rage to
purring contentment.

Even when we use words themselves, the manner in
which we say them varies greatly, with any number of implied meanings. Spoken with a tremor, the sentence,
"Your brother is coming home," could suggest fear.
Delivered with a sharp staccato tone, it could show disgust
or anger. The manner of delivery, the nonverbal message
of the sound, often carries as much weight or more weight
in communicating meaning than do the words themselves.
Yet these nonverbal aspects are inexact. We've all experienced misunderstandings in the communication
process. A large percentage of the time this is because the
subtext, the implied meaning, rather than the words themselves, is not understood.

In order to be truthful in a presentation, you, as an
actor, must understand the implications of every line of
dialogue. In addition, you must use your voice effectively.
Otherwise, you will not be able to communicate the
playwright's meaning to an audience.

The four aspects of voice usage are timing, volume,
pitch, and quality. Timing can be further broken down
into rate, duration, pause, and rhythm.

TIMING

Rate refers to the overall speed with which a speech is
delivered and can be measured by the number of words ut-
tered per minute. The determining factors of rate are the
emotional content of the material and the thought content
of the lines. A sad or reflective speech would be delivered
much more slowly than would one in which intense excite-
ment prevailed. A complicated speech would be delivered

at a slower rate than would something that is easy to follow and to comprehend.

Duration refers to the length of each individual sound, and, like rate, is dependent on the emotional effects desired and on the importance of the individual words. For example, if you were going to build suspense and an atmosphere of fear and apprehension, the rate would be faster than for a piece where the effect of each word is important.

Duration is also a means of emphasis, of highlighting a certain point. When analyzing a role or a speech, you should try to determine not only the important words but the thought centers as well. This means analyzing exactly what the character is saying so you know the important words and word groups. Determining what these are not only points out what is important but can show what should be emphasized.

The effect of a word or phrase can be heightened or pointed up by yet another device: **pausing.** If an actor pauses before a word, he or she is warning the audience to pay close attention. Successful comedians know the effect a pause can have before a punch line. Pauses also provide oral punctuation. It would be difficult for an audience to comprehend a selection that was read at an even rate. On the other hand, you should not pause every time there is written punctuation. If you do, the speech will be choppy.

Pausing, which also determines phrasing, is somewhat an individual matter and depends on three things: the author's style, the character's style, and the actor's style. It varies from situation to situation and depends on emotional and logical content.

The following could be delivered in several ways. Just two examples are shown, with one slash mark meaning a short pause and two a longer one.

O, pardon me,/ thou bleeding piece of earth,//
That I am meek and gentle with these butchers!//
Thou/ art the ruins/ of the noblest man
That ever lived/ in the tide of times.

O, pardon me, /thou bleeding/ piece of earth,/
That I/ am meek/ and gentle// with these butchers!//
Thou art the ruins/ of the noblest/ man//
That ever lived/ in the tide/ of times.

The last aspect of timing is **rhythm.** Any play should
have an inherent rhythm or rhythms. Of course, this
would be more apparent in the above excerpt from
Shakespeare's *Julius Caesar* because it is written in iam-
bic pentameter, or blank verse, which was the form for
Elizabethan tragedies. But rhythm, even in prose, involves
the recurrence of a word, an idea, a sound, or a pattern of
sounds. It can be found in such easily spotted devices as al-
literation, but more often exists in the flow of the language.
Many modern comedies, for instance, have a staccato
rhythm, whereas much of serious drama has a more state-
ly one.

VOLUME

Volume is determined somewhat by the mood and the
size of the audience. Anger might be conveyed at a higher
decibel level than would serenity. Like pauses, volume can
be used to point up or to emphasize. For example, the
words that should be spoken louder in the following are
italicized: What are you *doing* here? Can't you mind your
own *business?*

PITCH

An effective way of communicating meaning is pitch, or
changes in the frequency of sound. When a sound is

spoken at a higher pitch level than other words in a phrase, it has attention called to it. Go back to the example at the end of the last paragraph. Try to say the words in the two sentences at the same pitch level using only an increase in volume for emphasis. Now try to say the same two sentences by increasing the volume and raising the pitch level of the italicized words.

Changes in pitch not only occur from word to word, but within individual words. The latter, of course, is called inflection. A rising inflection can convey a question, a sense of doubt, or a sense of disbelief or shock. A falling inflection often conveys determination or certainty.

QUALITY

Quality, the remaining aspect of voice, refers to the changes in the overtones in one's voice when speaking. Changes in quality can be used to indicate changes in meaning, to portray certain emotions, or to indicate that a different character is speaking. Quality is most often associated with mood and feeling. For example, a gruff or husky quality may indicate an intense depth of feeling, such as sorrow, whereas a whining quality is often associated with pleading. The use of various voice qualities depends, to a large extent, on the actor's interpretation of the role or speech. In Garson Kanin's *Born Yesterday*, the female lead usually plays the stereotypical dumb blonde role with a slightly higher-pitched voice, suggestive of a dependent, little girl.

When experimenting with characterization, you may want to try as many variations in voice usage as you can, just so long as they are consistent with the content and the character.

To make sense to an audience, a speech has to make sense to the actor. In long or difficult speeches, it often helps to paraphrase, to write out in your words what the author means. Then you can try to come up with the style of delivery.

When you discover what you think works best for you, you can begin to make notes to yourself, similar to what has been done with the following lines from James Goldman's *The Lion in Winter*. First, the pauses are indicated and then the pattern of inflection.

At this point Henry is discouraged and bewildered, so the rate would be fairly slow, and there would be a hurtful bewildered quality to the words.

All my boys are gone.// I've lost my boys.// Oh, Jesus,//all my boys.

‾   ‾

‾ ‾ ‾ ‾ ‾ ‾ ‾

All my boys are gone. I've lost my boys.

‾

‾ ‾ ‾

Oh, Jesus, all my boys.

These lines were preceded by anger: "I deny you. None of you will get my crown. I leave you nothing and I wish you the plague. May all your children breach and die." Then the true meaning of his sons all turning against him sinks in. After that he switches once more to anger where the words might be more clipped and delivered with a sharper tone before he again lets the feelings of loss overwhelm him.

Exercises

1. Go through a well-known comedy and find an important monologue or speech. First, paraphrase it. Then experiment with ways of delivering it. Mark it for phrasing and inflection; determine the vocal qualities and rate.

Present the speech to the rest of the class. Do the same thing with a tragedy or serious play.

2. Through the use of inflection and variations in volume, give as many meanings as you can to the following sentences:

> a. "I just love walking in the snow."
> b. "Oh, that's wonderful, just perfect."
> c. "I don't believe I'll go with you."

Now write out two or three sentences of your own and pass them to a classmate to present in as many ways as possible.

3. Underline the key words in the following excerpt from Ibsen's *An Enemy of the People*. How would you emphasize them?

> Dr. Stockmann: (With growing excitement.) What does it matter if a lying community is ruined! Let it be levelled to the ground, say I! All men who live upon a lie ought to be exterminated like vermin! You'll end by poisoning the whole country; you'll bring it to such a pass that the whole country will deserve to perish. And if ever it comes to that, I shall say, from the bottom of my heart: Perish the country! Perish all its people.

Choose a monologue or speech from another play. Do the same thing, only make copies and give them to the other members of your class. Present the speech orally as they follow along. Have them critique your presentation.

4. Convey to the class the following feelings, states of being, or reactions, speaking only with numbers or nonsense syllables.

> dependency
> frustration
> disgust

accusation
nervousness
old age
sophistication
machismo
sneakiness
conspiracy
innocence
outrage

Have the class try to determine which you wanted to convey.

5. Quality, rate, and articulation are the most important factors in determining dialect or accent. Varying one or two of these can effectively portray area. Leaving off the final "r" in words can be characteristic of New England or the South. Generally, southern speech has a softer quality and a slower rate. Vary any of the three, slightly change the delivery of the vowel sounds, and you have a host of English accents.

Either through listening or library research, determine the characteristics of one of the following or any other of your choice:

Irish
Cockney
Mexican
Italian
West Indian
Russian
Norwegian
French

Now use what you have learned. Practice the dialect until you are confident you can do it yourself. Now teach it to a class member who has chosen a different dialect.

The Matter of Technique

THERE HAVE BEEN MANY systems and techniques of acting, from the beginnings of theatre to the present. Yet acting relies to a great extent on individual judgment and feeling. There is no right or single solution to how a role should be interpreted. There are many solutions, some better than others. To a degree the effectiveness of a portrayal depends on subjective judgment. We may dislike one person's style, while others find it truthful and captivating.

Of course, there are certain standards such as good vocal projection and intelligible speech. Yet one actor who is generally considered good may have a totally different approach from another who is considered just as good.

Acting is "good" if it is truthful. It is truthful if it fits the style of performance, supports and supplements the playwright's intentions, and is aesthetically pleasing. Beyond the basics, it does not matter much which approach we use.

According to Sir Laurence Olivier, acting is "the art of persuasion." "The actor persuades himself first, and through himself, the audience. In order to achieve that, what you need to make up your make-up is observation and intuition."[1]

Once Upon A Mattress, directed by William H. Zucchero at Kent State University (photo by C. James Gleason).

The audience is willing to be persuaded because they are willing to accept that theatre is like life. It imitates human experiences by allowing the spectators to identify with characters who are represented as real. The spectator then can put self in the characters' places and feel as the characters do.

As previously stated, actors bring their backgrounds and experiences to a production. They mold and shape these experiences into something new. They judge; they overlook; they point out specific traits to the exclusion of others because in the space of ninety minutes it is impossible to present a completely rounded character. The audience adds to what the actor has already added to, and so "accepts" that a character is three-dimensional, even though only a few traits can be explored during the character's time on stage.

The playwright and actors, and then the audience, select and, through this choice, add their own personalities to their perceptions of the world.

As an actor, you need to think and react as your character. You need to believe in the character as "I." However, some playwrights oppose this. Berthold Brecht, in rehearsing actors for his own plays, had them add at the end of lines: "he said," or "she said." For him the message, not the individual character, was important. He wanted audiences to identify with the problem, the theme, rather than with individual characters.

Brecht had a purpose in what he did, and many consider him one of the greatest modern dramatists. Still, his type of production was atypical. In the majority of plays, the actors do identify with the roles. Yet we cannot, as actors, empathize with the character's situation, especially in realistic plays, until we begin to think of ourselves as the character. Of course, we may still be able to give a credible performance, but it may have a hint of dishonesty.

In *Death of a Salesman*, we need to think: "I am Willy Loman, and I know I have been a failure," rather than "I am playing the role of a salesman who believes himself to be a failure." When we do the latter, we distance ourselves from the character. We ourselves are once removed, making the audience then twice removed. As actress Helen Hays says: "What you're doing on that stage is projecting yourself into someone else entirely, into the mind of the author, into the being of the character. You are trying to settle down to be comfortable in that character and speak the author's words. You are merely an instrument for what he is saying."[2]

There are two important points to consider in this quotation. First, the actress states that we should put ourselves "into the being" of the character. She does not say we should portray or play the character. Second, we need to think as the character, even while speaking "the author's words."

Although the lines in a play express meanings that you personally do not accept, and even though these ideas and meanings are said with words or word combinations that you yourself would not use, you have to make them natural to you. They are the character's words, which in turn are the author's words.

Writers often state that they either see their characters performing on a stage and thus are entities unto themselves, or that they "become" the characters as they write their lines and actions. The point is that if the playwright is being honest, the words are truthful. It is up to the actor to see that they remain so.

Maintaining Balance

In any stage presentation, there must be a combination
of empathy and aesthetic distance, more of one than the
other depending on the type of play. (See chapter nine for
a discussion of style). We cannot "become" the character
to the extent that we actually cause injury or death to
those who oppose us.

We operate on at least three levels. We are the character; we are our own personalities watching us "be" the
character; we are our analytical selves judging technically
and emotionally what we are doing. (This latter part of
ourselves is always present, even in our everyday lives,
evaluating what we do.) All this is further affected by the
actual audience or, during rehearsal, our **anticipation**
and **visualization** of the audience.

In addition, we constantly carry with us our private
audience, those individuals who have exerted influence
over us at some point in our lives and whom we still want
to please. We judge our own actions and accomplishments
in light of what we feel this audience would think. Often,
of course, their "advice" is outmoded. If so, we need to realize that what we are attributing to this audience is not
realistic, and the advice should be disregarded.

Communicating with the Audience

The audience should help us make a performance aesthetically pleasing. The audience affects us. Even though
we pretend not to be speaking to them, we, of course, are.
They are affected by what we do, which affects us. There is
constant feedback.

According to Ralph Richardson, "You're really driving
four horses." First is the "movements which have been

decided upon. You're also listening to the audience" and "keeping control over them. You're also slightly creating the part, in so far as you're consciously refining the movements and, perhaps, inventing tiny other experiments with new ones. At the same time you are really living, in one part of your mind, what is happening."

Richardson goes on to say that acting "is to some extent a controlled dream." "In one part of your consciousness it really and truly is happening. But, of course, to make it true to the audience, all the time, the actor must, at any rate some of the time, believe himself that it is really true."[3]

Not only do the performers' attitudes and actions change, but the audience changes as well. Each brings new expectations and attitudes, resulting in a different feedback loop from stage to auditorium. The live presence of actor and audience has a great effect on each. As actor/director Philip Burton once remarked: "Unless an actor is able to present a truly imagined and felt character, he is unlikely to hold an audience, but there must always be a part of him instinctively sensitive to his effect on the audience and ready to spring into action when he feels he has lost or is losing them."[4]

If a production slips too far toward empathy, it lacks artistry and, very likely, meaning. The participants become too involved and thus often cannot be separated from life. There have been many instances throughout history of audience members "coming to the aid" of actors. On the other hand, if the participants, audience, and actor are too detached, the play will have little or no application to life and so will be lacking in meaning.

How much an actor should "become" the character is a question that has never been satisfactorily resolved. Obviously, if actors totally lose their personalities in the characters, they will lose any sense of judgment and perspective. If they think or feel as their character to the exclusion of all else, in all probability they will begin "living" the character rather than delivering written lines and performing staged actions.

Approaches to Acting

There are two basic approaches to acting, the internal and the external, but they are not mutually exclusive. Whether they admit it or not, actors have to be aware of both; they have to draw from both, no matter what their training and background. According to Michael Redgrave:

> It would be not unfair to say that there are, roughly speaking, two kinds of actor: those who primarily play for effect and those who, whether by instinct or method, seek for cause before making their effect. But even this cannot be elevated into a dictum, for those who play primarily for effect— or as we say in the theatre, "from outside"—are by no means unaware that they must indicate, and to some extent feel, the cause or motivation which should precede that bid for effect. Similarly those artists who try to discover primarily the truth of a character are also usually aware to some extent of the effect they are creating.[5]

THE INTERNAL APPROACH·

Although elements of the internal approach had been practiced previous to Constantin Stanislavski's work with the Moscow Art Theatre, he is credited with bringing these elements together in his System of Acting. Opposing those styles of acting that relied on memorized gestures and posturing to portray each emotion, Stanislavski felt that dramatic truth should be presented through an observation of life. He taught that actors should seek truth of feel-

ing and experience in the characters they play, finding the
psychological depth of each role.

The Russian director, who founded his system in 1906,
believed that the secret of art was in discovering creativity.
He wanted to find its true nature in the human being and
subsequently discover the means for its development. He
became increasingly interested in the operation of the subconscious and the emotions, certainly aware of the work of
Sigmund Freud, who was dealing with the same principles
in treating his patients.

Stanislavski felt that an actor needs to move, perceive,
concentrate, and feel while on stage. He or she cannot
merely pretend to do so. Thus the internal approach involves feeling and relating emotions, thoughts, and ideas to
their outward manifestation.

THE EXTERNAL APPROACH

Although more actors in the United States seem to follow the internal approach to acting, the external approach
is still taught in much of Europe. Here the actor is concerned largely with technique. Rather than finding it necessary to understand emotionally what a character does or
says, it is necessary only to determine what the emotion is
and then modify outward, observed signs of the emotion to
fit the role.

For instance, when you are impatient you may constantly glance at your watch, look up and down the street, and
so on. Actors who follow the external approach would take
these actions and mold them to a particular role.

Critics of this approach say that the actors are using
"tricks" to present their characterizations, in that they are
concerned with effect rather than feeling. Yet to a degree
all acting involves tricks because the actors should be

aware of and play to an audience, and actors who begin
"externally" can then draw the feelings inward.

Although they lean more heavily toward one approach,
actors of necessity use a combination of the two approaches. And even though they "feel," the actors behave
differently in an onstage situation than in a similar situation in life. In a given situation it might seem more natural
to mumble or speak softly. But as Helen Hays says, "You
must share everything with the audience."[6]

The "dominant mode of acting" in the modern theatre
"has been some modification of the Stanislavski method"
where the actor "ceases to be a player representing someone else and is transformed into the character."

But while this has been the dominant acting style, the
reactions against it have been constant and extreme:
Brecht trained the actors in his *Berliner Ensemble* to
remember always that they were on stage playing a part,
and actors at the Abbey Theatre in Dublin, it is said, were
frequently rehearsed in barrels in order to restrict their
movements and to force them to concentrate on speaking
their poetic lines, thus reminding them that they were no
more than voices for the poetry, necessary but ultimately
unimportant instruments of the author.[7]

In contemporary theatre, methods of acting have
changed even further. Part of the experimentation can be
credited to the Living Theatre of Julian Beck and Judith
Malina, who believed that new methods should be discovered for new plays. Part of what they did was to try to
convince the audience that the events of the play actually
were life, rather than merely a representation of life.

Another important figure in contemporary theatre is
Jerzy Grotowski, who with his Polish Laboratory Theatre
tried to give the actors a technique based on total discipline, thus freeing the body and mind completely. He

believed that the best approach was to strip theatre and acting of all nonessentials. There should be no sets, makeup, lighting, or costuming. The actor, through discipline and control, should create these accouterments in the minds of the audience. By controlled movement the actors create whatever they wish the audience to perceive. Impulse and reaction are simultaneous. The actor does not merely desire to perform a certain action but is incapable of not performing it. The skills become involuntary. The goal is to eliminate mental, physical, and psychological blocks. The result is the totally disciplined formation of a role in which all inhibitions are nonexistent and every phase of self is revealed.

Again, the approach itself does not matter. What matters is that the actor bring an integrated self to the role. He or she must be willing to immerse self in the creation of a characterization. There must be no holding back, but rather the actor should use whatever facet or part of self is necessary to give verisimilitude to the performance.

Exercises

1. With a classmate plan a three- or four-minute scene, taking characters from a well-known play. Develop your character "externally." That is, figure out what outward signs or manifestations of his or her feelings would be logical in the excerpt you are planning. Now take these manifestations and adapt them to the type of character you are playing. Rehearse and present the scene. Afterwards, analyze and tell the class about your own feelings while doing this. Was there any point at which you actually began to feel the character's emotions? Did you ever view the character as "I?"

2. Now, with the same classmate, choose a scene of three or four minutes from a different play. Develop your

role using the internal approach. Was there any significant difference in how this made you feel? Was either character more "truthful" or "honest" than the characters in the external approach? Why do you think this? Were there moments you felt more like the actor playing to the audience than like the character living in the universe of the play? There should have been, especially if you were paying close attention to positioning, voice projection, and so forth.

NOTES

1. Hal Burton, *Great Acting*, 23.
2. Roy Newquist, Showcase, (New York: William Morrow & Co., Inc., 1966), 204-05.
3. Hal Burton, *Great Acting*, 71.
4. Philip Burton, *Early Doors*, 165.
5. Michael Redgrave, *The Actor's Ways and Means*, (New York: Theatre Arts Books, 1953), 13.
6. Newquist, *Showcase*, 205.
7. Alvin B. Kernan, ed., *The Modern American Theatre*, (Englewood Cliffs, NJ: Prentice-Hall, Inc., 1967), 16, reprinted from Alvin B. Kernan, ed., *Classics of the Modern Theatre*, (New York: Harcourt Brace Jovanovich, 1965).

The Script

I N ORDER TO EFFECTIVELY analyze a script and a role, you should be acquainted with the different genres, which have a great deal to do with the way the play is presented. You also should be acquainted with play structure and style.

Genre

Genre refers to the way playwrights treat their subject matter. The treatment is related to their outlook, which in turn affects the purpose in writing. What is depicted should be the truth of the human condition as the playwright sees it.

Overall, there are two broad methods of treating subject matter: serious and comic. Genre in itself is not particularly important. What is important is the success of the play, whether it is to ridicule and change something or to present a nostalgic view of the past.

Closely related to genre are the representational style and the presentational style. The former contributes to empathy, the latter to aesthetic distance. An audience can be reached by making them feel what the character is feeling. A play that leans heavily in this direction is serious in na-

Scene i

Setting: (*The action takes place in the living room of MELVIN and DENNIS' house in La Jolla. SR is a secretary desk, polished to a high gloss, in front of a bay window. A marble fireplace at the rear has never felt the heat of a match but rather has bleached driftwood lying on its shiny grate. The living room suite is white. A sofa sits SL and a chair just Right of the fireplace. End and coffee tables are scattered about and on the walls are various paintings, done mostly in shades of blue and grey. The floor is covered with a deep-pile carpet of blue. A few feet Left of the fireplace is a coat closet. UL of the sofa is a door leading to the rest of the house.*)

At rise: (*Melvin is seated in the chair near the fireplace. Because he is still recovering from a serious coronary, he wears felt slippers, silk pajamas and a velour robe. He is reading the L.A. Times. DENNIS enters UL and crosses to the couch. He wears khaki work pants and sneakers and a brown turtleneck. It is early evening.*)

MELVIN: (*Shaking newspaper to straighten the pages*) Every time I read the newspaper it scares me to death.

DENNIS: Then why don't you just stop reading it? (*He flicks imaginary dust off the back of the sofa, circles it and sits.*)

MELVIN: (*Surprised*) What?

The first page of an original script on which the director and actors will make notations showing stage directions and possibly indications of character development.

ture. On the other hand, the audience can be approached
through the intellect. Comedy is funny because of aesthetic
distance. In real life, a man's tripping over a rock and
breaking a leg would not be funny. In a comedy it might
be. The reason is that we do not closely identify with the
leading characters in most comedies. We keep our aesthetic distance. A way of looking at the difference between
the two is to think of a raging fire. If we see it on television
and know it was set to test firefighting equipment, it can
have a certain beauty. But if it is burning down our house,
we are affected emotionally. The first instance does not affect us personally; the second does.

Most plays are neither pure presentation nor pure representation but a mixture, which allows people to identify
with the characters and feel their emotions. At the same
time it stops them from running onto the stage to help out
when a character is in difficulty.

TRAGEDY

The most basic genre for serious treatment of a theme is
tragedy. The playwright wants the audience to identify
completely with the protagonist, who after struggling
against overwhelming odds is defeated.

Tragedy deals with human nature at its most basic: the
struggle between good and evil. Tragic protagonists either
battle a flaw in themselves or evil in others. The forces are
always more powerful than they are. But through defeat
they remain noble and in this respect are triumphant.

We feel compassion and share in the suffering. We
grieve at the tragic hero's defeat. At the end we should experience a release of emotional tension, a catharsis, that
leaves us at peace. We have identified with a noble character, a human being like ourselves. Therefore we must to a
degree possess the character's nobility and positive traits.

When the protagonist pursues a goal to the end, we feel the same strength and persistence in ourselves. If the character is good, we too have the capacity for goodness, reaffirmed by the protagonist's noble battle. Above all, tragedy reaffirms our faith in ourselves as part of the human race. Even when tragic characters die, their heroism lives. It is not their deaths but what the playwright says about life that is important.

The working of the protagonist's mind is the most important aspect of a tragedy. The playwright makes us feel we are experiencing the struggle and death of someone close to us. Although they are good, tragic heroes are imperfect. Because of their weaknesses, we can relate better to them.

Tragic heroes face the consequences of their actions and realize that they will be defeated. But along the way they gain new insights into themselves, as should the audience.

COMEDY

The opposite of tragedy is comedy. Whereas tragedy is a fairly narrow form, comedy has the greatest variety of any genre of drama. It can be slapstick or gentle. It most often shows a deviation from the norm of everyday life, even though it often is concerned with the mundane and the pettiness of day-to-day living.

The writer may want to have us take ourselves less seriously or to free us from tension, even if just for a couple of hours. The playwright often reminds us of our own frailties but is telling us they are not so serious as we sometimes think. Another purpose of comedy may be to correct social injustice. The idea is that if we can laugh at social and character flaws, maybe then we will be more inclined to correct them. In this way comedy is corrective.

The humor can come from the treatment of character or situations. Any subject matter can be used if it can be treated in a humorous light. If the deviation from the norm becomes too painful or too severe, the comedy stops being funny. It would be cruel to treat physical deformities or handicaps as sources of comedy. It is the things over which we have control or our views of uncontrollable forces that comprise the subject matter.

Such things as eccentricities of character can be humorous, as is Moliere's treatment of Harpagon's greed in *The Miser*. Other character traits that might be the basis of comedy are hypocrisy, laziness, or overwhelming ambition.

Comic protagonists may become involved in situations with which they are unable to cope or that are outside their knowledge and experience. An example might be a plumber posing as a diplomat. Comedy ridicules our tendency to be what we are not or to place too much importance on our involvements and our goals.

In comedy the protagonist has to win. Otherwise, the audience would feel guilt or shame for having laughed at the character. So it is important that a comic frame of reference be developed. If the audience is not given this frame of reference, they may not know how to respond. The spectators should know that what they are seeing is not to be taken seriously and that they are not expected to identify either with the character or the situation, unless it's a matter of laughing with instead of at the protagonist.

MELODRAMA

Melodrama combines some of the elements of comedy with those of tragedy. It is similar to comedy in that it most often has a happy ending. It is related to tragedy in

that it treats a serious subject and the audience identifies
or empathizes with the characters. But unlike tragic
characters, those in melodrama are one-dimensional.

Melodrama often relies on creating feelings of terror,
and coincidence or fate plays a large part in the outcome.
Good always triumphs. The form includes sentimentality.
It is often episodic in that the most exciting events and
situations are included in the script. There also is comic
relief in the form of the minor characters.

FARCE

Farce is similar to melodrama in that fate often plays a
part in the outcome. But it is more closely related to comedy, and its main purpose is entertainment. It uses
stereotyped characters who are completely one-dimensional. The plots, which are highly contrived, rely on physical actions and devious twists. There is never any
important theme, and the progression shows only how the
major characters manage to release themselves from en-
tanglements.

Although farce often deals with illicit sexual relationships and infidelity, its outlook is amoral. The aim is only
to provide laughter for the audience, and much of the fun
is in the visual gags and absurdities of speech. The plot
relies on misunderstandings. Often there is physical
violence, mistaken identity, and deception. The characters
are victims of their vices and appear ridiculous when
caught.

TRAGICOMEDY

Tragicomedy mingles elements of the comic and serious.
The term is paradoxical in that a protagonist who is truly
noble cannot appear comic, nor can a comic protagonist

possess the scope of a tragic hero. Nevertheless, some
playwrights do mingle comic and tragic. Often a situation
appears comic, but later the audience realizes it's serious.
Tragicomedy generally tries to show how life intermingles
the comic and the tragic.

There are plays that do not seem to fit any particular
genre. Some, such as *A Raisin in the Sun*, possess more
scope than melodrama, yet do not end in the protagonist's
defeat. Sometimes three-dimensional characters are
presented in plays that are neither tragic nor comic, as is
the case with *The Glass Menagerie*, which deals with
people who are trapped by circumstances and their own
limitations. During the course of the play, the characters
are not defeated. Instead the defeat has started long before
the play opens.

Style

Style refers to the way a play is written and designed.
The representational style attempts to imitate reality, and
the audience empathizes more fully with the characters
and the situation. The presentational style, on the other
hand, is audience-centered. It proclaims that theatre comes
from life but definitely is not life.

Style is just a basic approach to a play or a production,
and none is pure. Every play is a mixing of two or more
styles, but the style of the production and that of the script
have to match. There are some plays that demand a particular approach, while others can be done in a variety of
basic styles in production.

NATURALISM

The most representational style is naturalism, which attempts to present life as it actually is. In pure naturalism an attempt is made to include everything found in life. In writing this means including all the details of conversation and physical movement. In setting it means including everything that would be found in an actual dwelling or location. Even those things that are never used by the actors have to be real. All windows have to open, all fireplaces work, and all costumes match those in everyday life. Method Acting, based on Stanislavski's System, often was ridiculed because many of its practitioners misinterpreted what the Russian director had written and tried to make their acting duplicate life. They mumbled, failed to project, used annoying mannerisms, and so on. Often those who acted in this manner were said to be of the "itch and scratch school."

Of course, there can be no such thing as pure naturalism because everything in life can't be exactly duplicated for the theatre, nor can life exist onstage as it does outside the theatre.

REALISM

Realism is close to naturalism in that an attempt is made to convince the audience that what they are viewing is life, although realism is selective in that it does not include every detail. Anything needed to convey a mood or atmosphere or to portray character can be included, whether it is actually used in the play or not. Realistic dialogue is made to sound like that of life except that it is more selective with less extraneous detail and more direction. Another difference between naturalism and realism is that although details may be included to convey mood or

character, they needn't be the actual object nor do they
need to be practical. (That is, the windows do not need to
open or guns really be capable of firing unless called for in
the script.) The objects seen onstage should appear to be
just like those in life, although they can actually be substitutes.

EXPRESSIONISM

A style that is more audience-centered but still has some
elements of the representational is expressionism. The
central character is seen as his or her inner self. The setting relies on the script to provide the answers to how the
protagonist views life. This viewpoint then is expressed in
the setting. In other words, the audience is made to see
reality as the protagonist sees it.

IMPRESSIONISM

Impressionism deals with the design of the set, exclusive
of any conditions demanded by the script. The designer
and the director figure out what they want to stress most
in the setting, and this element is applied externally to the
production. Impressionism is usually selective in what is
shown. It is, in effect, the director and/or designer giving
an impression of the play.

SYMBOLISM

With symbolism, the playwright presents life allegorical-
ly for conveying any message or sense of truth. The set
likewise is more presentational than that of many other
styles and doesn't attempt to portray a realistic view of life.
Often, undefined forms are used only to give a general im-

pression that will convey the playwright's message. Generally, the acting is more "poetic," less tied to life.

Structure

Plays are structured in a number of ways. The most traditional is the cause-to-effect or story play, which still draws the largest audiences.

THE STORY PLAY

From the time we are small, we learn to like stories. When we think of them, we generally think first of being entertained and second, perhaps, of learning something. Stories are interesting because they usually deal with people in situations with which we can identify. In books and plays our interest is maintained through our anticipation of the outcome and how it will be accomplished. A story holds our attention because of its unfolding and its revelations. In other words, the plot keeps us in suspense.

Plot involves the meeting of opposing forces. Their struggle continues until one of them is overcome. One is the protagonist, the other the antagonist. The former is the central character who needs or wants to reach a particular goal; the antagonist opposes him or her. The protagonist generally is an individual, though in rare cases it can be a group. The antagonist is another person, a group or a non-individualized force such as social or economic conditions. It may be the protagonist's environment, the forces of nature, or even a condition within the mind, and it is shown largely in the central character's relationships with others.

The story play begins with a particular situation in which there has been balance, or else the balance has been

upset shortly before the action begins. At any rate, until
the beginning of the action there has been no great difficulty for the characters. Then the **inciting incident** occurs
and the balance is destroyed. A question is raised that
must be answered. This introduces the **rising action**.
During this period, the protagonist's problem is intensified
through a series of complications. The suspense increases.
Will the protagonist finally triumph or be defeated? The
suspense, the struggle, and the conflict continue to build
until the action can go no further without something ir-
revocable happening. This means the **turning point** of
the play has been reached. Now the protagonist knows he
or she will win the struggle against all opposition or else be
destroyed. The actual point at which the central character
wins or loses is the **climax**. The remainder of the play is
devoted to the **falling action**, also called the denouement.

Sometimes the turning point and the climax are the
same; at other times they are separate. Suppose two men,
the protagonist and the antagonist, are fighting. One
decides that the only way to win is to kill the other man.
The point at which the decision is made is the turning
point. The actual killing is the climax. If the decision is carried out instantaneously, the turning point and the climax
are the same. If the protagonist decides to kill the antagonist but feels it would be better to wait until a more op-
portune time, the turning point and the climax are
separate.

This is the basic structure but it is oversimplified. The
story actually may begin long before the play opens, but
the playwright does not include all the events preceding
the inciting incident. Instead, we learn any important
details through dialogue. In effect, then, the story includes
much more than the play, which usually covers a short
span of time.

The writer needs to decide the **point of attack**, the place to begin the play. It should begin as close to the climax as possible or the play tends to become boring.

In most plays, however, the action does not build in a straight line to the climax and then fall off for the unraveling or the reestablishment of the status quo. Instead the plot involves a jagged line where a series of minor crises and struggles are introduced as part of the overall problem. Sometimes these minor problems seemingly are resolved, only to intrude again and complicate the rising action. For example, in the musical *The Fantasticks*, the first act ends with Matt and Luisa prepared to live happily ever after. Then the second act opens with each of them being dissatisfied with life, which each feels the need to experience further before settling down. So a problem—concerned with their spending the rest of their lives together—apparently has been solved by the end of the first act, only to be complicated further at the beginning of the second.

The complications in all but the simplest of stories result in a series of minor climaxes that can be compared to a fencing match. First, one person attacks and drives back the other; then the second attacks and drives back the first, over and over again at increasing intensity until one is declared the victor. Each of these minor crises somewhat alters the direction of the play. Each is introduced by one minor climax or resolution and ended by another. But the frenzy or suspense continues to build. It changes from speech to speech and from scene to scene.

Even in scenes where there appears to be no conflict, it is inherent; it relates to what already has been shown. It may reveal character or show the workings of the protagonist's mind. An example is Hamlet's "To be or not to be" soliloquy.

Plot refers to movement, or progression, and to action. The plot is made up of scenes, which may be defined as units of dramatic action. Without these, there would be little interest in a play except possibly for the uniqueness or originality of the setting or situation. Action is what gives the play its life.

Dramatic Action

Dramatic action is related to the opposition of the protagonist and the antagonist in moving the story forward. It needs to be motivated by what has preceded it.

This is not to imply that forward movement must be restricted in any way simply because it does not *seem* to contribute to the overall plot. Maybe it accomplishes another valid purpose that indirectly helps to advance the plot. Often, a character is individualized in the eyes of the audience by some repeated action.

Dramatic action must relate in some way to the central character. Even if this person is not present, it must concern or be initiated because of him or her. To build the series of minor crises and climaxes that hold the interest of the audience, the central character must initiate action that in turn affects him or her. Once the characters act, they must expect to be affected by their behavior. Dramatic action involves a clash of forces and is always reciprocal. It can be compared to communication. If you say hello to someone, that person usually says hello to you. If you argue with a friend, you can expect an argument back. But if you are talking to a group of people in a formal situation, they usually don't have the option of answering directly, although you do receive feedback in the form of facial expression and body language. The same thing occurs

among characters in a play. Nobody in a play is in his or
her own personal limbo. All the major characters are
responsible for everything they say and do. As an actor,
you have to be aware of what your character is thinking at
all times and what his or her purpose is in the unfolding of
the plot.

Even when one character seems to dominate, there is an
interchange of action. The other person is acting, though
maybe not as forcibly. If this were not so, or if there were
no feedback, the play would lack meaning. Perhaps the
person who is being dominated is slowly building up a
resentment that will be acted upon later.

Each minor complication or each change in action involves a revelation of character. We learn a little more about
the central figure in a play by what he or she does when
opposed. The character is then presented somewhat differently in each scene, and it is up to the actor how to show
this, besides through the lines.

The audience wants to know what the character really
is like. Does the person live up to their expectations? Because of what the protagonist does, will he or she triumph?
Or be defeated? *How* will this happen? Without dramatic
action always occurring in the present tense, there would
be no play.

After the climax should come the falling action, that
part of the play that shows the results of the previous action. The climax begins to show the answer to the question
asked when the problem was introduced; the falling action
finishes answering the question. It may answer more fully
how and why a certain thing happened. It may show the effects of the resolution on the characters. At any rate, it ties
up all the loose ends. An example is the "Requiem" scene
in *Death of a Salesman*.

Other Types of Structures

Another type of structure is thematic, that is, a play is unified around a particular theme. It may have a multiplicity of scenes all dealing with the same basic issues but unrelated to each other in continuity or characterization. Obviously, there would not be as much empathy on the part of the audience, but on the other hand, the message conceivably could be brought out in a more straightforward manner than would be the case with a story play. The drama that relies on theme for unity often is episodic with various situations dealing with the same subject but taking place with different characters in different locations. Or it might be like some of the **absurdist** plays that deal with a single set of characters. An example is Thomas Beckett's *Waiting for Godot*. Many such plays show no real progression of events but do bring home the message of lack of communication or nonawareness.

A play may be presented just to portray a facet of life or a way of life. One such play that has strong characterizations but no real cause-to-effect plot structure is *The Effects of Gamma Rays on Man in the Moon Marigolds*. It deals largely with the relationships among a mother and two daughters. Such plays often present a vignette or an impression, or maybe the writer just wants to express a viewpoint of life and have the audience compare it with theirs.

Sometimes plays without a plot show incidents following each other in chronological order but not necessarily growing out of the preceding material. In this way they differ from the story play.

Script and Character Analysis

SCRIPT ANALYSIS is an involved and lengthy process. The director is responsible for all facets of a production, so his or her analysis is broader than the actors, who nevertheless have a lot of work in figuring out character.

The Director's Analysis

The director analyzes a script to try to understand the writer's meaning before the actors begin their interpretation of character. The director's first job is to determine the theme or purpose, whether it is a reexamination of something everyone knows or the restatement of a universal truth.

Theme is also tied closely to how the playwright wants the audience to feel after the final curtain. Maybe the writer wants to call attention to something important, maybe to reexperience an awareness of a particular problem of society or to look more closely at their own values. Often, theme is no more than an observation of life rather than a concrete statement.

The Fantasticks at Marquis Public Theatre (photo by W. Tritten Robin).

The director has to be sure the production style matches the writing style. If it doesn't, the audience will be confused.

As they work with the script and later the actors and designers, directors may change some of their concepts. Still, they work out the largest portion of the analysis alone.

Directors sometimes try to develop a metaphor that is carried out in the design and acting. In the original design for *Cat on a Hot Tin Roof,* Maggie and Brick's bedroom resembled a boxing ring because they were always fighting.

For a better understanding of the play and the writer, directors often research the historical period, the locale, and the writer's life; this research is not a bad thing for an actor to do as well. It may provide glimmers of understanding not obtainable in any other way.

After deciding upon the overall concept, directors become more specific in their analysis. They figure out which elements of the play are most important for the audience's understanding and which are least important and can be deemphasized. Many times directors will add elements, both in design and movement, to emphasize a particular facet, such as characterization or circumstance. Hokey business, for instance, sometimes is added to farce to point up its silliness. Usually, depending on the director, the actor is free to try to add whatever he or she feels is fitting and adds to the overall communication of the theatre experience.

The director has to decide the basic action or the areas of conflict in the play as a whole and in each scene. Where does the major climax occur, and how can it be pointed up? Where are the minor climaxes in each scene, and how should they be presented? Much of this has to do with focus, deciding who and what are most worthy of attention in any particular scene.

Next the director determines the prevailing mood or atmosphere. Is it basically nostalgic or comic, tragic or sentimental? There are subtle or abrupt changes in mood throughout a play, but there is a prevailing atmosphere or feeling that is most important to the script's message.

Directors as well as actors determine how each character relates to the play as a whole and how the characters relate to each other. According to director Alan Schneider, "a play is a series of relationships" and "dramatic action, to me, means a change in relationship."[1] Directors determine why each character is included and how each advances the theme. What struggle is the most important in providing the play's dramatic movement? What needs or desires do the characters symbolize? How is each character unique?

During the analysis a director also thinks in terms of setting and technical elements. What type of environment will best portray the atmosphere, mood, actions, and circumstances? What elements of design are necessary? At some point in the planning, the director meets with the designers to present these ideas. Some directors prefer to work out the total design concept themselves, whereas others are open to suggestion. In the same way, some allow actors much more freedom than others do.

After approving the set design, the director considers how much blocking to plan before the show is cast and rehearsals begin. As a general rule, directors work out the broad movements but leave the subtleties of gesture and characterization to the actor, who spends much more time in analysis of his or her specific role. Experienced actors are likely to have a sense of what is right for any situation, and directors may prefer to give them more freedom than they give beginning actors.

The director deals with the overall production and has
the final say regarding any artistic aspect. But the actor
has much more responsibility for his or her own presentation.

The Actor's Analysis

An actor approaches a new role by what is referred to in
the Stanislavski System as seeking the **spine** or **super-objective**. Each character can be thought of, in the context
of the play, as having something to be achieved. The super-
objective is this goal. It is expressed as an action and not as
a feeling or emotion. (A play also has a super-objective,
which is synonymous with central idea. It is the direction,
or where the dramatic action is leading.) The super-objective of a particular role cannot be anything like: The
character wants to be loved. An emotion is a state of being
and cannot therefore be acted. Rather, the goal could be
stated as: Mary Jones wants to entice Robert Smith into
falling in love with her.

In *Death of a Salesman*, Willy Loman's super-objective
could be that he wants to gain success, which he defines as
having money and being "well liked." Toward this end he
deludes himself into thinking that he is a great salesman
and finally commits suicide so his sons will have the
money from his insurance policy.

Defining the spine works best with realistic or naturalis-
tic plays whose characters approximate real people. One
actor conceivably could discover a different spine for a role
than another actor. For instance, Willy's super-objective
could be: Willy Loman wants to be loved and respected by
his sons. In order for this to happen, he feels, he must be a
financial success.

After determining the super-objective, the actor analyzes each individual scene to figure out its specific objective and how it relates to the character as a whole. The goal in every scene may differ, but each contributes to the overall goal, the super- objective.

Material about a character is provided in dialogue of the other characters, in lines the character delivers, and in the character's actions. We learn much from the way others in the play view a character. The setting also can tell us about the character's present circumstances.

Character, of course, is one of the most important aspects of a play. The type of character chosen by the playwright often determines the environment. To a large extent, even the situation is prescribed by the characters since any person placed in a specific set of circumstances will react to those circumstances in a different way than will any other person. In your analysis you need to figure out how your character is feeling and what his or her purpose is in each scene. Much of this is not apparent; it is most often not stated. Rather, much of it can be discerned in the **subtext**, what is being said "between the lines."

Exercises

1. Figure out the super-objective of a play with which you are familiar. Now take a character from that play and figure out his or her super-objective.

2. Break one of the acts into scenes, defining "scene" as "unit of action," ending in a minor climax. Figure out your character's objective in each scene.

3. Try to determine the overall or prevailing mood of the play and the mood of each of the scenes for which you have determined the character's objective.

4. Choose one of the scenes to present in class, a scene in which there are two or, at most, three characters. Figure

out your character's relationship with the other charac-
ter(s) in the scene.

In everyday life, as you learned, more than half the message we receive in any direct communication is presented
nonverbally. The subtext, the implied meaning, often tells
us more than the text. It is up to the actor to determine the
meaning over and above what is actually stated in words.
This meaning depends a great deal on the individual
character.

Character is that element of a play with which the
audience most closely identifies, so except in nonrealistic
plays, it is that facet of the play or production that carries
the most weight. (There are exceptions. In some plays
character is deemphasized and audiences empathize with
the plight of an entire group of people or with a social condition.) Because an audience feels empathy or sympathy in
a play, you need to be as certain as you can that your
analysis is correct or logical.

KNOWING YOUR CHARACTERS

None of us knows how he or she will react to a new
situation. We can only guess. The same is true of the
characters in a play. As the analysis and rehearsal
progress, we learn to know them better.

It helps to know much more about the characters than
ever will be revealed in the play. What will cause them to
flare up or back down? If they are threatened, will they
retreat or will they lash out? Are they easily defeated, or
will they accept no defeat? The text and subtext should tell
you.

Characterization can be compared to a building that has
many sub- levels. Only a small part of the total building is

visible, just as in life only a small part of a person's psychological makeup is revealed to others. Similarly, a large portion of the character is buried below the surface, but there is a depth from which to draw. Because of a character's background and experiences, he or she will react believably, but differently from another character in any situation. To have the characters appear to an audience as three-dimensional, complete human beings, it helps to know them as well as you can by the time of performance.

You need to examine your character's psychological basis and background. Usually you'll discover that if the playwright has done his or her job, the speech and actions are logical outcomes given the character's "past."

CHARACTER ANALYSIS

Knowledge of a character does not come in a flash but is a slow process, just as it is a slow process to learn to know someone who will later become a friend. Certainly, you form first impressions of other people, but these impressions often are not lasting. You have to know people longer than a few minutes before you can begin to understand their personalities. You learn to know characters in a play by analyzing them.

First determine the characters' physical attributes and what makes them individuals, different from others of the same general type. It is obvious that the physical appearance over which a character has some control, for instance, hair style, clothing, and makeup, will follow a certain pattern because of the character's feelings and attitudes about life. You need to figure out the how and why of these psychological aspects.

Know the characters' backgrounds. Where did they grow up? Were their families poor or wealthy? How did the economic situation affect their outlook? How much schooling have they had? What are their interests and hobbies? What kind of work do they do? Are they happy with their jobs or would they rather be doing something else?

What kind of speech patterns do they have? How is their speech affected by the location where they grew up, by their schooling, or by their present environment? How does their speech reflect their personalities? What is their vocal quality?

How are other people likely to view them? Not just the other characters in the play, but others in their universe. Would they be liked? Why, or why not?

What were the biggest influences in the characters' lives so far? What in their backgrounds has caused the biggest changes in their outlook? Are they optimistic or pessimistic, introverted or extroverted?

What beliefs and attitudes do they hold? What brought about these beliefs and attitudes? Was their early background strict, or did their parents give them a lot of freedom? Did the parents care about them? What was their parents' relationship with each other? How did parental attitudes, habits, living conditions, and environment affect them?

Are your characters moral persons? What do they hope to accomplish in life? What are their main goals, both in the context of the play and overall in their lives? What are their drives? How do they define success? Are they envious of others? Are they bitter toward life? How are they likely to act in any given situation?

All of these questions and any others you can think of will allow you to know and project your character as a three-dimensional individual, not as a cardboard caricature. Much of this information will be part of the exposition; the rest is up to you.

Next you need to examine the relationships among the characters. What do they think and feel about each other? How do they react to each other?

Creating characters is a subjective process. Often those we create are different parts of ourselves, tied as closely to us as they are to the playwright who originally conceived them.

DETERMINING THE DOMINANT TRAITS

You need to decide what traits of your character are most important for the audience's understanding of the play. Even though you know your characters fully, the audience cannot. There just is not time. And so they have to appear simpler than people in real life so the audience can easily grasp what they are like. If you try to show too much, the character may come across as vague.

In everyday life we learn to know people by seeing them acting and reacting to their environment. We learn about them by the way they meet crises or handle conflict. We discover the most, for instance, about Walter Younger in *A Raisin in the Sun* by seeing him in conflict with the neighborhood representative. This confrontation shows facets of his personality that were previously buried below the surface. But, as an actor playing the role, we have to figure out an effective means of showing the most important aspects of his personality in this particular scene.

When characters are opposed in any way, we learn more about their emotional and psychological characteristics. When the opposition becomes the strongest, the most important qualities will be revealed. Reactions to crises or conflict may reveal things the characters did not even realize about themselves. In these moments, actors portraying these characters have to be the most convincing.

Exercises

1. Take the same play you worked with previously. Write a biography of the character whose super-objective you defined. Include what has been established by the playwright as well as other traits that are consistent with this and that help you or the audience understand the character better.

2. Figure out the character's most important traits in the context of the play. Are they the same as his or her important life traits? Why or why not?

3. Work with a classmate and present a five-minute scene from the play, showing the results of what you determined in Exercises 1 and 2.

REVEALING A CHARACTER

It is a common misconception that the central character of a drama has to undergo a massive change or a personality reversal. Such a change is not logical. Personality has been determined by a human being's entire background, so it is not reasonable that one major crisis should cause him or her to reject all that has gone before and undergo complete psychological and emotional change. Your character can undergo an emotional catharsis, but his or her personality remains basically the same.

Instead of massive change, we have character revelation. A part of a character's personality that was not apparent previously is revealed in each new situation. The revelation occurs gradually throughout the play. If the audience were to see the total character at the beginning of the first act, they would have little interest in the play's outcome. Any revelation must be logical in view of personality and background. Some of this, of course, depends on the writing; much of it depends on its depiction.

Characters may change their minds or their courses of action or even their goals. But such changes are brought about by something already inherent in their personalities. The changes result only from seeds already growing, which maybe even the characters themselves failed to recognize. An actor has to be able to portray this evolvement realistically.

Even if a character is defeated, even if the person commits suicide or is driven insane, the potential for that suicide or insanity must be there before the event actually occurs. For example, in *Death of a Salesman*, Willy Loman commits suicide, but his death comes as no surprise.

Exercises

1. Read a modern play and figure out everything you can about the background, physical aspects, and personality of the central character. Has the playwright made the person believable? How could the character be better presented?

2. Read a play and determine the basic needs of the characters. Try to determine if these needs are logical.

3. Choose a tragedy and analyze the reasons for the central character's defeat.

4. Read a comedy and compare the central figure's dominant personality traits with the tragic character's dominant traits.

5. Develop a character that could be the central figure in an original play. Write a detailed analysis of that character. Analyze goals, needs, drives, and motives, as well as background, current situation, personality traits, and physical appearance.

Many times actors find that their analysis does not work. Then they need to discover why. Maybe the analysis was incomplete or even wrong. Maybe the interpretation just cannot work for one actor but can for another. Maybe it doesn't fit in with the director's interpretation. Sometimes, at their own instigation or that of the director, actors will completely change the entire characterization.

Building and growth often seem to occur naturally once actors appear on stage together. It is much easier to act well yourself when your fellow actors are doing their best in presenting their characters. When all perform together, it is easier to set the mood and to determine the rhythm and pace of the play as a whole.

NOTES

1. Joseph F. McCrindle, ed., *Behind the Scenes: Theatre and Film Reviews from the Transatlantic Review,* an interview of Alan Schneider by Jean Claude van Itallie, (New York: Holt, Rinehart and Winston, 1971), 279.

The Integrated Actor

YOU ARE IN A VULNERABLE position as an actor. Each time you audition for a role and do not get it, you in effect are being rejected. Or at least a part of you is. Certainly, in many cases it is not your fault. You simply do not match the director's vision of what the role should be. Then no matter how good your interpretation nor no matter how well you present yourself, you will not be cast.

When you immerse yourself in a role, again you are leaving yourself more vulnerable than ever. You are putting yourself and your abilities on the line.

If something we do not care much about is rejected, the rejection doesn't matter to us; the hurt is less. But when we do care, we are open to hurt.

When you are not chosen for a role, it's good to remember that the director is not rejecting the whole, integrated person you are, simply the immediate manifestation.

Success does not usually come without failures. Although a cliche, this statement is true: we learn by our mistakes. If we nurture our hurt or fail to consider that in a particular instance the director is right, or if we fail to think about a critique of our work, we cannot grow.

Tobacco Road, directed by Louis O. Erdmann at Kent State University (photo by C. James Gleason).

Ego is very much involved in any of the arts; no matter how gently others critique our work, we often feel hurt, even when we know what we've been told is for our benefit.

Because imagination and creativity are such fragile parts of our being, when we first begin to act or write or paint, it is best to gain confidence without criticism. We are ready for critiquing only when we are more certain of ourselves and our abilities and when we see those abilities are similar to those of others. Of course, the person doing the critiquing should be gentle. Not everyone is.

When being critiqued, take into consideration that the critic may not be right; he or she has different views and expectations than anyone else and thus different opinions; ego may demand that he or she look good, and one way of making self better is by tearing others down.

If you allow it, criticism can be disastrous. There was the case, for instance, of a recent college graduate who had a short story published, which a novelist friend then told him was worthless. He continued to write—twenty-six book-length manuscripts in twenty-six years, all stored in footlockers, never read by anyone else. All this because of one harsh criticism!

Then there was a young man who had his first professional role in a summer stock theatre. For some reason the director had it in for him. In front of the rest of the cast, he tore apart everything the actor did. The director even went so far as to have the understudy go through several hours of rehearsal, threatening to let him take over the role. To the actor's credit, he continued to do the best he could when he resumed rehearsal. He played the role instead of allowing himself to be crushed. Then twenty, he went on to become the host of a popular television talk show. Had

he allowed the criticism to defeat him, he certainly would
not have the success he enjoys.

Becoming Successful

Each role molds and shapes you. You are influenced by
it, not only in the performance but later. Each role, each experience adds to your insight, your capability as an actor.
You mold the role to suit your talents and personality; the
role, because of what it requires, molds you. You reach into
your being and draw out what will help you communicate.

When you immerse yourself in the part, when you concentrate, when you study human nature, then you do your
best. And this is what success is. It is making your characters memorable and believable.

After the analysis, another way of making the character
real is to talk with him or her in much the same way you
might interview a local celebrity for a feature story in the
newspaper. You spend time with the person. You ask questions to bring the person into sharp focus. The character
interview can help you expand and grow. You can use it to
develop an established character or to create a new character. The reason for making the established character real
is obvious. There are many reasons for starting from
scratch. First, it helps you define more clearly the facets of
human nature you may need to draw upon in a role.

This is how the interview works. Someone agrees to be
"it." Classmates either in turn or at random ask whatever
questions they want. There are three rules for the person
being interviewed. First, there should be no advance planning. Second, the actor should not answer as self but as an
emerging (or scripted) character. Third, all answers must

be consistent. In this instance, we will take a totally new
character.

Suppose the person on the "hot seat" is an eighteen-
year-old male from Brooklyn.

Q: How old are you?
A: Thirty-two.
Q: Where do you live?
A: In Ohio.
Q: Oh, really? What part?
A: Near Columbus.
Q: Do you like it there?
A: It's okay, but my job's a dead end.
Q: What do you do?
A: I'm senior editor with a small publishing company.
But we're going under. And I'd really like to get out.
Q: What do you want to do?
A: I have this dream, you see. I want...

It's best to let each question grow out of the preceding.
Establish a time limit, a minute or two, but make sure you
carry out the process long enough for a complete character
to emerge.

Of course, you can do the same thing with a character in
a play. Take Willy Loman, for example.

Q: What do you want most out of life, Willy?
A: I want to be successful. I want people to like me.
Q: Why is that important to you?
A: That's what everyone wants, isn't it?
Q: I just want to do my own thing. I don't care if
people like me or not. Why do you care?
A: I want the respect of my family and my friends. I
want my boys to look up to me. Every man wants to
be a hero to his boys.

Q: That's how you would define success, then? As
being liked or respected?
A: I suppose. Maybe that's part of it. But, good Lord,
man, everyone knows that success equals money.
Q: That isn't always true. How about discovering a
cure for cancer, or...?
A: I can't agree with you there.
Q: What do you mean? Aren't those things important?
A: Of course they are. But they're going to make
somebody rich too, aren't they?

In the character interview, you, the actor, can play both
roles if you wish, much the same way a novelist or
playwright might create original characters.

A second method for developing character involves word
association and works just as well in establishing character
traits—either physical or personality. For example, you
might say the word "stingy" and without hesitation name
another trait, such as "needs recognition." These could be
followed by "sixty-two," "male," "effeminate," "loving,"
and so on. Now take a certain number of the traits, possibly four or five, and write a thumbnail sketch of a character.
Add whatever you wish to what you already have. You can
write a straightforward description similar to the following:

Bill Simpson is sixty-two, has green eyes and dark
brown hair. A loving person, he nevertheless is stingy.
Effeminate in actions and appearance, he's principal
of the junior high school in a small town in Northern
Kentucky.

Or you can place the character in a setting:

Johann Benson, a bank executive, is sixty-two years
old. Many people have grown to hate him in the com-

munity where he lives. This has to do with his stingi-
ness, which carries over into his reluctance to approve
loans at the bank. He makes people feel uncomfortable, almost criminal.

Or you can begin right away with a situation:

Johann Benson, vice president of the First National
Bank of Euclid, Pennsylvania, sits at his desk, chewing nervously on the skin of his lower lip, already raw
and ugly-looking. The owner of P & P Construction
Company, Paul Peterson, one of the most influential
men in town, is coming in to demand a loan. And
Johann is the type of person who cannot stand con-
frontations.

You can write it in the form of a script if you wish. It
matters only how you approach the character sketch, only
that a believable person begins to emerge. Also, when
you've done the word association, you can decide to use
only certain traits, being free to add other facts as you go
along. In other words, be flexible.
    You should know physical characteristics, background,
attitudes and beliefs, patterns of behavior, and dominant
traits.
    These are all related. A person's educational, psychologi-
cal, and emotional background affects his or her attitudes
and behavior. It is your job to go into detail about your
character to make the person believable to yourself as well
as to an audience.
    You may want to develop a character from an individual
trait (again either an original character or one in a script).
Suppose, for instance, that you begin with a middle-aged
female character. Let's take just one aspect of that character, her speech. How was it affected by the location where

she grew up, by her schooling, by her present environment? What sort of effect do these things have? How does her speech reflect her personality? What sort of vocal quality does she have? From here, go on to every aspect of the person's background and present circumstances.

The more completely an actor understands the character, the greater the communication with the audience. In a sense, this means being in the character's mind, seeing events and circumstances from his or her point of view. As the creator of a character, you have to realize that while you are acting, it is the character who is the center of the universe, not yourself.

Now is the time to make good use of the exercise of seeing through another's eyes. Spend an hour or an evening as your character, experiencing the world through this person's point of view. You learn how your character reacts to a variety of circumstances and stimuli.

Or you might try the idea of reacting to an object or experience as your character and then as yourself to help point up differences and understand more fully the character you're developing. Walk as your character; sit as the character. Do all that you can as the character. Then pay particular attention to how you do them as self and what the differences are, both in the physical actions and how they make you feel.

Exercises

1. Observe on four successive days a girl, a boy, a man, and a woman—people you don't know. Maybe you can watch them in a shopping center, a sidewalk, or a restaurant. Write a character sketch of at least half a page about each, using actions as well as physical appearance. Try to determine what kind of person each is. Then

develop an environment and a situation in which to place the characters.

2. Write out the traits you would find most desirable in a friend. Now develop a character based on these traits. Do the same thing with traits you would find undesirable. Put the two characters together in a scene in class or let them talk to one another on paper.

3. Write a one-page character sketch of the most interesting person you encountered today. What makes the person particularly interesting?

4. Write various snatches of conversation in which the following characters are revealed:

   a) a snob
   b) a kindly grandfather
   c) a genius
   d) an abusive spouse
   e) a concerned parent
   f) a half dozen character types of your own choosing

Then agree to be interviewed in class as one of these characters.

5. Using one of the conversations you have written, fill in actions and descriptions of the people involved as well as the location.

6. Write another scene in which character traits and personality are revealed through actions rather than dialogue. Rehearse and perform a scene based on this character.

7. Take at least one of the characters who has begun to emerge as a result of any of the previous exercises. Now write a complete character analysis of the person. Then place him or her in a logical environment, but one that is different from any of those above.

8. Develop a character based on someone you know. Develop another character completely in your imagination, perhaps through word association or the character interview. Now put these two together in a scene and have them talk to one another. Have them come into conflict with each other. Write the scene. Perform it with a classmate.

9. Try once again the exercise of listening to a short conversation and extending it in your imagination and on paper. Fill out the scene, using whatever elements you need—setting, character description, and so on.

When written down, these exercises provide you with a record you can go back to when building characters in the future. You can also keep a record of people and behaviors you observe. Write down traits as well as actions. By this you can learn much about human nature. Whether or not you use any of these people as the basis of a character, you have taught yourself to be aware of what people are like in a variety of situations.

The exercises that follow are similar to earlier exercises; they will help you feel emotions and physical characteristics. Here, however, you are to apply the results directly to a character.

Exercises

1. Assume a certain posture and determine how it makes you feel. Why does it make you feel this way? Describe the sensations and the mental changes. Create a character from these new feelings.

2. Smile, frown, grimace and so on. Hold the position for a time. Describe how you feel. What character could feel this way? What sort of situation would the person be in?

3. Along the same lines, mirror the expressions of others and come up with a character.

4. Imagine the next stranger you see as having a stuffy nose. Describe the person incorporating this trait in the description. Do the same thing with other traits.

Improvisation

THE CHARACTER INTERVIEW is close to improvisation, which is helpful to an actor for many reasons. In an unscripted situation, it forces actors, if they are being honest, to see the truth of a character. Whether beginning with a totally new character or working with a character from a play, it is important to be faithful to the character's personality and experience.

When the director asks a cast to improvise with the characters in a play, it may add new dimensions to the roles or show how the character would behave consistently in scenes outside the written play.

For example, it might help the actor to experience something referred to but not actually included in the script. In playing Biff, the elder son in *Death of a Salesman*, the actor might improvise a scene where he is caught cheating on a test. Thus, he can experience the anger, the shame, the disappointment that led him to Willy's hotel room.

A director also may have actors improvise a scene totally unrelated or very loosely related to the action of the play. This allows the actor to get a more rounded picture of the character, to remain faithful to him or her, and to understand how traits revealed in the script can affect outside events.

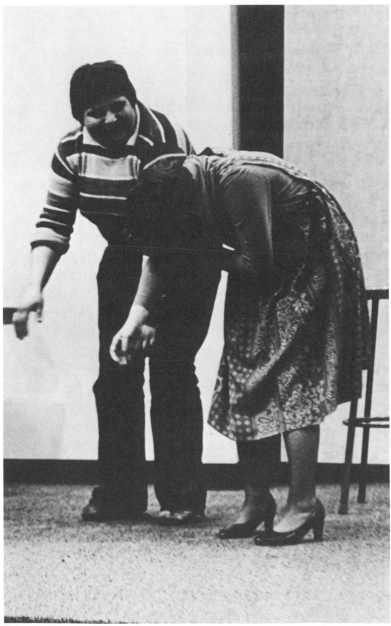

Students doing improvisation in an acting class at Edison State
College in Ohio (photo by Kathy A. Oda).

Improvisation is beneficial for a number of reasons: it requires concentration and total attention; it necessitates thinking and reacting as someone other than self; it requires awareness of human nature and of specific situations and their effects.

Sometimes actors in a play become stale. That is, they fail to continue to live the character, but rather perform by rote. This happened when Donald O'Connor played the role of Felix in *The Odd Couple* on Broadway. His responses became automatic, like a robot's. He stopped listening or paying attention to the unfolding of the play. He went so far as to pause for a few seconds on expected laugh lines. Because he was not giving himself to the performance, he failed to communicate the humor. Thus, during these pauses there was silence instead of the laughter he expected.

An actor needs to approach a role in every performance as if it were a new experience, because it is. The character does not live the same experiences over and over. He or she lives them only once. Improvisation during the run of a show can help bring back the spark to a character because it forces the actor to think in new situations as the character.

The purpose of improvisation is to help you, the actor, in developing your skills or improving a specific role. Therefore, improvisation should not be approached with dread or trepidation. Rather you should look upon it as a chance to learn and grow as a performer or a character.

If you approach improvisation in this manner, you will see that you can be in control, that your character does have a life, that you can establish contact and communicate with the other actors on a truthful level. But it is important to be certain you really hear and follow what is going on. In everyday life, most often we do not worry

about the next response we will make, as we sometimes
tend to do in improvisation. Rather, we listen and respond,
or, if we are bored, change the subject or the action. But we
do not usually worry about it beforehand.

Most often in an improvisational situation, you have
given circumstances, just as you do in a play. This
means that certain things have been established. The situation has been set up ahead of time. It can be an elaborate
preparation or the bare essentials, which the performer is
free to add upon but *not* change.

Given circumstances include any background necessary
to the understanding of the situation, the scene, or the
plot. It may include such things as setting, geographic location, financial status of the characters, historical period,
and so on. The actor, both in a play and in an improvisational scene, needs to follow through with whatever has
been established.

Thus, if you are given a situation and motivation for a
scene, you execute these intentions as precisely as possible.
The scene should not ramble. Often, inexperienced actors
will get themselves into an improvisational situation they
cannot handle. So they begin to change their characters to
make the situation easier to resolve. What often happens is
that the scene still rambles until it simply peters out. You
should beware of this. If you try to remain in control, to
concentrate, and to be faithful to the character and the
situation, generally this can be avoided.

In preparing for improvisation, you need to take a few
moments to assess the given circumstances and to decide
on the important facets of the characters or the scene that
are not given. You then need to examine the why and
what of the situation and analyze the goals of the character in this specific situation, just the way you would in a
scripted play.

The following should help you get started in improvisation. They begin with simple vignettes, then progress into scenes that should have an actual high point or climax.

Exercises

1. Listen to and record one side of a phone conversation. Based on what you heard, write out the other side. Now extend the conversation on paper another two minutes. Finally, write a thumbnail sketch of the people on each end.

2. Observe a stranger, on the sidewalk, at a shopping center, or in a store. Create a background for the person based on what you see and what you can surmise. Be consistent. Now write a thumbnail sketch of the person. Based on what you have done, think of a logical situation in which to place him or her.

3. Try to find one or two unusual or distinctive traits about everyone with whom you come into contact within the next twenty- four hours. Using one person and the trait(s), begin to develop a character. Write a biography or put the character in a situation. Read it to the rest of your class.

4. Visualize a blank page in a notebook. Now imagine a word or phrase on the page. Use it as the basis of a characterization.

5. Think of five people you have seen during the past twenty-four hours. Now do role-playing, assuming the personality of each. Then write out a sentence for each that begins: "I am the sort of person who..."

6. Each person should bring a common household object, such as a screwdriver, a magazine, a dish, and so on, to class. The class should sit in a circle so everyone can follow the entire exercise. In turn, each object should be

passed around the room. React to each object as one of the characters you created in the preceding exercises.

It is important to remember in doing any improvisations that you do not need to try hard to be original. It is better to proceed without mental blocks. Do whatever comes to mind. For instance, take one of the objects brought to class by someone else for exercise six and say the first thing about it that comes to mind. If you hesitate, discuss with the rest of the class why you think you did so.

In improvisation, often the more obvious you are, the more realistic and appropriate or original you appear.

Finding the Intentions

A play or a scene, especially in a play with a plot, involves a character meeting an obstacle, simple or complex. As you have learned, the play itself has a super-objective or spine. But within each unit of action the obstacle or the goal may differ yet contribute to the overall problem.

Not only does the protagonist want to reach a goal, but so do the other characters. The antagonist's goal is the direct opposite of the protagonist's because they are struggling against each other. Even the minor characters, to a certain degree, have to encounter conflict.

Each character has a certain purpose or action to perform in each scene. Figuring out intentions means determining reasons for each bit of action, for coming up against each obstacle. For example, at the end of Act I, Scene ii of *The Lion in Winter*, Henry offers Eleanor his arm before they go to another part of the castle for a Christmas party. One of his lines states: "We have a hundred barons we should look the loving couple for." So

it apparently is easy to discover the intention behind what
he does.

Yet both Henry and Eleanor are devious; they constantly play games with one another. Despite the fact that
Henry answers "no" when Eleanor asks if he ever loved
her, the two characters have a true affection for each
other. The actor playing Henry must interpret the intentions of the scene. It may be that they simply are preparing
to play a loving couple in front of others. But why would
they really care what they others think? Henry has
Eleanor imprisoned and lets her out only for the holiday.

An actor might decide that Henry actually does care for
or even love Eleanor, but he loves power more. So the intention could then be paradoxical in his offering her his
arm. The lines state this is a pretense. Yet even though
both Henry and Eleanor are constantly struggling for
power, for gaining and keeping the upper hand, they do
respect each other. So there is caution in what they do, as
well as acknowledgment of the other's capabilities. Besides
that, both are afraid to relax their guards even for an instant. And they probably do have affection for each other.
At the same time, Henry is too proud to show Eleanor that
he is at all worried. Therefore, to a degree, he is blustery in
his approaches to her.

In light of all this, the actor's intention in offering his
arm might comprise a complexity of reasons, all of which
much show in the way he performs the action. In the
majority of scenes, the intention probably will not be so
complicated. In an earlier chapter, we discussed different
ways of playing Henry. So, of course, there are different interpretations of the scene.

Intention is the inner life of the character and the
drama. And in each scene it requires identifying the
obstacle. In the scene from *The Lion in Winter*, Henry's

obstacle is personified in Eleanor. At this particular moment he needs to show that in no way has he weakened. His intention in the scene might be to get and retain the upper hand in their relationship, which in turn contributes to his overall goal of retaining power and determining how the kingdom will continue to run.

Many times you cannot discover the intention just by reading the lines. You have to know the characters to understand their reasoning, their motivations, as well as their relationships and how they feel about the other characters. You need to start thinking as the character and listening to the character's inner dialogue.

Henry might state in this scene: "I want to keep the upper hand. To this end I refuse to give an inch or to allow Eleanor to glimpse any uncertainty I feel. But deep inside I'm a little bit frightened because I know her capabilities. I know how she has tried to thwart my plans in the past. I know she has schemes of her own."

Each of the intentions, each of the actions, contributes to the overall characterization, the constant revealing of personality to the audience.

According to Robert Lewis, "Intention is what you are doing on the stage at any given moment, regardless of what you are saying or not saying...When I say doing, of course, I mean doing *inside*. It is, in fact, your reason for being on the stage..." and can be "quite different from the obvious significance of the dialogue."[1] Sometimes it can match the literal meaning of the lines, but it often does not. Actually, it can be just the opposite.

For example, a character wants to coerce another into doing something. In the lines, she expresses her awe for the character so she can manipulate him. Actually, she feels only contempt. But she'll play the game of flattery simply to gain the ends she wishes. This is what happens in Moliere's *The Miser*, where Froisine tries to get Harpagon to agree to marry Marianne.

Your performance depends on how you choose and carry out your intentions. As Lewis says, "If you choose funny intentions, what you do is likely to be funny. You won't have to act funny."[2] But you will have to know the character.

Exercises

1. Determine intentions and actions and perform the following scene:

Setting: a street corner, early afternoon, summer.

Characters: a man and a woman in their twenties, casually dressed.

Action: the woman stands near the curb; the man stands in the doorway to a store. The man demands that the woman come to where he is. She refuses.

There can be many intentions, such as: the man feels faint and needs help. The woman doesn't know him and recently has been mugged. Or the pair is married, and the man wants to buy a pool table. The woman thinks they shouldn't waste the money, but instead should save it for a trip to Europe. Take the same scene and give the characters different backgrounds and motivations. Change the intentions and backgrounds once more and do still another scene.

2. Figure out a new situation, characters, and action. Chose two classmates to determine intentions and play the scene.

3. Work with original scenes you have written or your instructor brings to class. The instructor will then tell each

of you your reasons for behaving as you do. But he or she will not tell any other characters who will appear in the scene with you. Now perform a scene, really listening and paying attention to the other actor(s). Decide how your character would logically modify behavior as a result of what you discover as the scene progresses.

When doing scenes such as this, it is important to remain faithful to the character and do as the character would. Of course, you are free to add whatever personality traits you wish.

During the study of your lines, keep in mind how the underlying intention fits the character's super-objective. Usually, the super-objective has to do with trying to influence others. This is not necessarily an evil thing. In Ibsen's *An Enemy of the People*, Dr. Stockmann tries to influence others to have the contaminated baths closed down. He is opposed by those who feel that the baths should remain open and continue to provide a flow of money into the community.

You need to figure out not only what the character wants, but how far he or she is willing to go to achieve the goal. Stockmann will follow up on his convictions no matter what the results. So will Oedipus Rex in searching for the murderer of his father, even though all the evidence points to himself as the killer.

In a play, you as actor cannot create a character in isolation. During the rehearsal period you will find the character acting and reacting to what the other actors are doing with their characters. At times you may even have to change your intentions, depending on other actors' interpretations of their roles. Suppose you are playing the role of Eleanor in *A Lion in Winter*. Now take the same scene discussed earlier. Henry and Eleanor are about to attend the Christmas banquet. Just before Henry takes her arm, he tells her he is tired of war and wants a little bit of peace. She asks if he would like instead everlasting peace. Suppose Henry plays the role just as was discussed. The actress portraying Eleanor learns to play off him to react to his intention and adjusts her own intentions according to what he does.

Suppose now that the actor playing Henry has to leave the production. Instead of sparring with her, as our original Henry had, the new one acts genuinely hurt by what she says about "everlasting peace." He plays the scene as if he is trying to shake off the threat of what she has said when he offers her his arm. Then, of course, when she takes his arm, her intention would be different. Maybe now she feels a pang of conscience when she asks if he ever loved her. The lines and the basic situation remain the same, but the intentions do not.

Exercises

1. Acting, or situations in life for that matter, are often like games. We are involved in conflict and want to win. We want to achieve our objective. It can help to play a scene while playing a game as simple as tossing a ball back and forth. Play an improvisational situation in which you oppose another character while you play a game of volleyball over either a real or imaginary net. Then figure out other physical games to play while doing other improvisations.

Even if you lose the physical game or the game taking place in the scene, you do not lose overall. As mentioned in the early chapters of this book, creating should be joyful. So, in creating your character, if you have done your best, you should have an inherent feeling of joy, which certainly makes you a winner.

2. Analyze a role in a play. Then do the following:

a. For the next few hours walk, sit and perform all your usual activities as if you were your character.

b. Wear an article of clothing neither you nor your character would normally wear. Spend the next hour or two as your character. How are the character's feelings different because of the clothing? What does this tell you that you might be able to apply to the scripted facets of the character?

3. Spend a whole day as if you possessed a certain physical trait you do not possess. In what way does this change your views? Now do the same, pretending you have a specific personality trait you do not possess. For instance, if you are outgoing, pretend that you are shy, or vice versa.

4. Plan a group improvisation in which all the characters except one suffer from the same physical ailment, another in which all except one are very heavy, very thin, and so on.

5. Perform an action that one of your classmates determines. Now figure out a character who would normally perform this action. Provide a background and intention. Present the same character in a scene of conflict. Have your classmates determine if the character was a logical outgrowth of the action. Why or why not?

Now develop a background for a character and perform an action. From what you have done, your classmates should figure out the sort of background you envisioned. For either of these the action should be fairly short and simple. For instance, a person going into a bakery to buy a pie; someone sweeping a floor, and so on.

Which of these two opposites is the easier to do? Why? Discuss this in class.

6. In the novel *Voices in Time*, the author Hugh Mac-Lennan sets up a situation in which most of the world's population has been destroyed, along with most technology. One of the characters discovers a sort of time capsule containing diaries and video recordings left by his relatives before the destruction.

First, do an improvisation in which you, as the viewpoint character, are looking at these objects from decades earlier. What sorts of things do you discover? How do you treat what you find? How does it affect you?

Now do a group improvisation in which you are of the new generation that has no memories and little knowledge of this past world. React to the diaries and video recordings you find.

7. Think of three nouns, such as car, bee, and oil lamp. Do an improvisational scene with one or two other people in which these three words become an important part. Think of other trios of words and perform improvisational scenes incorporating them.

8. Decide upon any object, such as a chair, a book, or a box of tissues, and build a scene from it. Use the object, making it an integral part of what you do. Yet never refer to it in words. Simply perform actions as a result of using it.

9. Develop a set of given circumstances. Tell the rest of the class what they are. Now with someone else do an improvisation using them as the basis. When you are finished, use the same set of circumstances to develop a different scene or to go a different direction.

10. Develop another set of circumstances and perform an improvisation with someone else. When the director calls time, freeze right where you are. Switch positions and roles and take the scene to a logical conclusion.

11. Bring a photograph or a print of a painting to class. Trade with someone else. Now develop given circumstances directly related to the picture. With someone else, present an improvisational scene that is a direct result of what you saw and developed.

12. Do some character interviews. After each one, two *other* class members should present an improvisation derived directly from the interview. It may be based on the character that developed or on others the character referred to. You may even simply take circumstances he or she mentioned and use them as your basis.

NOTES

1. Lewis, *Advice*, 54.
2. Ibid., 65.

Rehearsal and Performance

T HERE ARE SIX STAGES of rehearsal, which can last
from four weeks in professional theatre to six weeks in
educational and community theatre.

READING REHEARSALS

For the reading rehearsals the director often prefers a
relaxed atmosphere where the actors feel free to discuss
the script. Reading rehearsals are somewhat misnamed.
The usual purpose is to agree on the script's interpretation. At the first rehearsal the director may have the actors
read through the play to grasp the overall concept, without
attempting to develop character. Or the director may read
the script aloud or have someone else read it to insure that
the actors pay attention to the play as a whole, rather than
worrying yet about establishing character or interpreting
lines.

At some time during the reading rehearsals, the director
may show sketches and floor plans to the actors so they
can visualize what the set will be like. Most important, the
director discusses his or her interpretation of the play with
the actors and listens to their ideas.

Two actors rehearsing a scene in *Sugar,* directed by Jill Lynn at Little Theatre of Tuscarawas County.

The director usually explains the effects he or she hopes to achieve and the interpretation of the play's central idea. The actors and the director should come to understand the basic action and motivation, why the characters behave as they do, and the goals of each. Only after this is the cast ready to move to the stage or rehearsal hall to work out movement and business.

BLOCKING REHEARSALS

Movement is planned just after the reading rehearsals but continues to build and change throughout the rehearsal period, just as characterization continues to develop.

CHARACTER AND LINE REHEARSALS

From the time of the first rehearsal and sometimes even earlier, the actor will begin working out a character interpretation, which in turn influences how the lines will be delivered. Then after the blocking rehearsals, the actor begins to concentrate fully on the development of the role. The director tries to free the actor from inhibitions about establishing a character or experimenting with the character's development.

During this entire period the character should grow. Occasionally, the director will have to provide guidance for the actor who has failed to understand the style of the play or the intricacies of the character.

FINISHING REHEARSALS

The action of the play, the characterizations, and interpretation and the delivery of lines are refined and polished during the last part of the rehearsal period. Up to now the director has stopped scenes when necessary and corrected blocking and line delivery. The actors have had elusive lines provided. At this point, unless something is really wrong, the rehearsals proceed without stopping and without the actors using scripts. This way the actors gain a better sense of the script's meaning and the way that it plays. Often it is not until this time that an actor can fully appreciate the impact of a role. At the end of each rehearsal or just before a break, the director will give notes to the actors.

TECHNICAL REHEARSALS

By the time the finishing rehearsals end, the performance aspects of the production should look pretty much as they will during performance. Out of necessity, during the usual two or three technical rehearsals, the director will devote attention to the technical aspects of the production, neglecting the actors. Often a stage manager takes care of the runs-through from this point through to the production of the play.

DRESS REHEARSALS

The dress rehearsal is a tryout of the production, much as a Broadway theatre tries out the production either in the theatre where it will be presented or out of town.

There are usually two rehearsals in full costume with all the technical elements. Directors sometimes invite outsiders so that the actors can become accustomed to playing to an audience. During long runs, additional rehearsals may be necessary when certain roles are re-cast.

During the dress rehearsal and performance, the actors have added dimensions of costumes, makeup, actual properties, and the set itself, which often seem to bring the play completely to life.

The Performance

During the run of a play the actor maintains and perhaps even grows in the character, without straying from what has been rehearsed. There are probably as many ways of doing this as there are different actors.

Certainly, you'll need to keep up your concentration during a show's run. One way is to be prepared each evening for your entrances.

Many actors like to get to the theatre early so there is plenty of time to prepare for the performance. Then they can sit quietly, go over their lines, or concentrate on characterization.

During the show itself, it is a good idea not to become involved in all sorts of other activities backstage, which can remove your thoughts from the play and the character. Before each entrance you might want to do a few stretching or relaxation exercises, both with your body and your voice.

Some actors take a few minutes to get into the proper mood for the scene; some follow the play's entire action so that they will not be tempted to get involved in other things.

A performance is when all the preparation, learning, and rehearsal pay off; it is the climax, as it were, of all we have done as actors.